Happier Parents, Happier Children, Happier World

Graeme J Schache

Co-author

Alison Roberts-Wray

Also by Graeme J Schache:

Leadership for Outstanding Results
ISBN 978-0-980337662
Published 2008

Published by Graeme J Schache, co-author Alison Roberts-Wray

Copyright © Graeme J Schache & Alison Roberts-Wray 2015

The National Library of Australia
Cataloguing-in-Publication Data

Schache, Graeme & Roberts-Wray, Alison
Happier Parents, Happier Children, Happier World

ISBN 978-0-9923002-3-4 (pbk)
ISBN 978-0-9923002-4-1 (epub)

1. Families
2. Communication in families
3. Domestic relations
4. Parenting

646.78

The Authors of this book accept all responsibility for the contents and absolves any other person or persons involved in its production from any responsibility or liability where the contents are concerned.

All rights reserved. No part of this publication may be reproduced, stored in a retrieval system, or transmitted, in any form, by any means, electronic, mechanical, photocopying, recording or otherwise, without prior permission from the author.

Typeset in Constantia 12 pt

Produced by TB Books
        P.O. Box 8138
        Seymour South Victoria 3660
        Email: info@tbbooks.com.au

Cover Design by Pam Collings TB Books
Cover Photos by Shot at Close Range
Illustrations by Jessica Collings
Paperback available from www.planetearthparenting.com

DEDICATION

Fifty years from now the world will be better because you were important in the life of a child.

We dedicate this book to all the families who are striving to make the world a better place for their children.

Contents

Dedication. v
Acknowledgements ix
Chapter Summaries. xiii

Chapter 1: Introduction. 17
Chapter 2: Learning to Learn. 21
Chapter 3: Listening. 33
Chapter 4: Moods and Emotions. 56
Chapter 5: Knowing Ourselves; Knowing Our Children. 79
Chapter 6: Caring For Ourselves; Caring For Our Children. ..113
Chapter 7: Raising Girls. 131
Chapter 8: Raising Boys. 143
Chapter 9: Bonding and Relationships. 157
Chapter 10: Conversations for Stories and Assessments 176
Chapter 11: Conversations for Possibilities. 201
Chapter 12: Conversations for Co-Ordinating Action. 213
Chapter 13: Identity. 243
Chapter 14: Reflections. 256

References & Recommended Reading. 262
About the Authors. 266

ACKNOWLEDGEMENTS

I, Graeme, have taken a lifetime to realise that my calling is for all the people in the world to be happier (and more peaceful). At one point I set a goal to have an impact on world peace in my lifetime but I couldn't figure out how I was going to do this. Being the sort of person I am, and with the work I do in the corporate world, I started to think about approaching it from the top down.

Then one day a customer and friend, Peter Dewar, gave me a book, *Parenting for a Peaceful World* by Robin Grille. *Ah ha*, I thought, *I get it. I am starting at the wrong end!* So I embarked on trying to find who might be interested in playing with me re this, to no avail. So I parked the idea for a while.

Then another friend, Desley Lodwick, who I least expected to be interested in parenting, contacted me to see if I would be interested in working with her on parenting! My first thought was the universe works in strange ways and that this must be something I have to do. Desley introduced me to Alison Roberts-Wray who has worked as a primary school teacher and who is also very interested in parenting and its challenges. We did a workshop facilitated by Robin Grille. Conversations led us to realise we all wanted to have an impact on the earth and its future, with a focus on people being happier and more peaceful. So the three of us formed PlanetEarth Parenting.

The very first people I would like to acknowledge are Peter Dewar for being the messenger and showing me the way, and Robin Grille for his insightful workshop and his fabulous books. I then wish to thank Desley Lodwick who restarted me, and Alison Roberts-Wray who became my co-author. This book would not be the book that it is without the truly valuable input from Alison and the great conversations that we have had over the duration. Alison and I now look forward to growing PlanetEarth Parenting as business partners.

I would then like to especially thank my wife, Jan, for her support all through the project. I would also like to acknowledge my three sons plus Adam, who I have had close relationships with for all their lives, for providing me with wonderful experiences that have provided material for this book. I would then like to thank my grandchildren as subjects to also observe. I would especially like to thank my youngest grandson, Cooper, for being such a delightful subject to observe for the first three years of his life, and while this book was in its gestation period.

I, Alison, would like to thank my partner, Tom, my son, daughter and family for their love and support. I would also like to thank all the parents and children I have worked with for enriching my life.

It would be very remiss of us not to acknowledge the work of Fernando Flores, and to Julio Olalla and Rafael Echeverria for originally teaching Graeme the Ontological interpretations which are included in this book. Subsequent to this Desley and Alison have also completed studies in this work in Australia. We also acknowledge the generosity

Acknowledgements

of Shaun McCarthy and Peter Geyer for allowing us to use some of their work in this book.

In addition, I wish to thank Jenny, Bertie and Samantha Grayling for their exceptional ongoing generosity in allowing me to spend so much time in their beautiful holiday home near the beach, which is such a magical place for me to retreat to in order to do my writing.

We thank Daniel Schache and Caitlin Ogilvie from Shot At Close Range Photography for the concept and production of the photos for this book and other PlanetEarth Parenting materials.

Finally, we thank Jessica Collings for her talented work on the illustrations, and Pam Collings at TB Books for putting this book together into a professionally presented text.

CHAPTER SUMMARIES

Chapter 1: Introduction

Happier Parents, Happier Children, Happier World is designed to enhance family relationships, develop new ways of observing, new understandings and new ways of parenting. A focus throughout the book is on how to parent each child according to whom they are so that they can be the best person they can be.

Chapter 2: Learning to Learn

Chapter 2 discusses barriers to learning, the four domains of learning and how these relate to developing a unique style of parenting that meets the needs of each child.

Chapter 3: Listening

Chapter 3 defines the act of listening as one that involves our five senses combined with our interpretation of that listening. It outlines the three 'A's' of listening and demonstrates how to listen to, and understand, each other more effectively.

Chapter 4: Moods and Emotions

The authors identify common human moods and emotions and discuss the difference between moods and emotions. They describe the impact of moods and emotions on who we are, how we react and act, and demonstrate how we can change our moods and emotions.

Chapter 5: Knowing Ourselves; Knowing our Children

Chapter 5 develops the readers' knowledge and ability to better understand themselves and others. This understanding gives us the ability to accept ourselves and others, and use this knowledge to take care of our own and others' needs more effectively. This chapter offers outlines of the Myers Briggs Type Indicator and Human Synergistics Circumplex Styles as tools that help develop a deeper knowledge of ourselves and others.

Chapter 6: Caring for Ourselves; Caring for our Children

Chapter 6 offers insights into how to manage the well-being of ourselves and our children. It details the three domains of stress, managing stress and the impact of stress on conversations and relationships within the family.

Chapter 7: Raising Girls

Chapter 7 gives a deeper look at female-specific biological and social make-up, giving the reader a broader understanding of how girls 'tick'.

Chapter Summaries

Chapter 8: Raising Boys

In Chapter 8 the authors take a deeper look at what makes boys 'tick', and the risk of labelling boys who don't fit into our narrow definition of boyhood.

Chapter 9: Bonding and Relationships

In this chapter, the authors discuss the importance of strong family bonds on relationships, how to embrace one another's differences, have the difficult conversations and work towards a shared understanding of parenting.

Chapter 10: Conversations for Stories and Assessments

Chapter 10 is an in-depth look at this common style of conversation and its impact – both positive and negative – on our moods and our perceptions of ourselves and others. It shows how to recognise this style of conversation and use it effectively to manage conflict and relationships.

Chapter 11: Conversations for Possibilities

In Chapter 11, Conversations for Possibilities are described. Methods of how to use this style of conversation to shift negative moods and move towards a shared goal are outlined.

Chapter 12: Conversations for Co-ordinating Action

Mastering these conversations is critical for parents who want to make clear requests, gain commitments and set boundaries. This chapter has detailed information about the elements of an effective request, the responses we have to a request, managing commitments and complaining effectively.

Chapter 13: Identity

Chapter 13 shows the impact of a positive identity on how others see us.

Chapter 14: Reflections

This final chapter presents a summary and the importance of raising children to create a better future for our planet.

CHAPTER 1: INTRODUCTION

Our story is like so many life journeys. It started out with an idea, set off in a certain direction, made quite a few changes along the way and arrived (for now!) at a place that is a little unexpected, but a good place to be. While our philosophy, or our 'why we are doing this', didn't change, the pathways we took certainly did.

Our journey began with a conversation. We wanted to make the world a happier and more peaceful place. If we have happier parents then we will have happier children. Our children are the future and our purpose is to have them want to make the world a better place.

We want to make parenting easier and more enjoyable; when we refer to parents we mean anyone who is involved in raising children.

We believe there is no greater expert on your children than you. In this book, and through our coaching work, we can help you to better understand yourself and your children. With this clearer picture of how people 'tick', you will be more confident that your parenting decisions are the right decisions at the time. Parents really do have the most important job in the world.

This is a book to help you enhance the relationships with members of your family, develop new ways of observing yourself and the world and learn new ways of interacting with others. It is also for you to consciously discover what works for you and each of your children. This book is written to add to your current knowledge and skills in being with children.

We are well aware that any discussion or anything that we might read about parenting is a very sensitive subject. When reading this, please resist the temptation to be critical of yourselves and what you have done so far. We all do what we do given what we know at the time, and the past is complete. Even if you reflect on what you have done so far and assess you have made some mistakes, be mindful, not so much about the mistakes, but about the story you hold about them. We learn from our mistakes! The cars we drive today have evolved by the designers continually correcting mistakes. When a plane leaves an airport to go to another airport destination, it does not go in a straight line; there are continuous corrections of the flight path. What we are offering you is some additional knowledge. If you take one message from this book, it is the message of acceptance. Accept yourself as you are, understand who your children are and enable them to be the best they can be.

Each child is uniquely different, you are uniquely different, and each relationship is uniquely different, so what is written in this book is how to tap into that uniqueness. In our coaching of parents we work to help parents work out for themselves and with their children what is best for each member of their family. We do not coach from a position that we know what is best for you or your child. We claim we are all different observers of the world, and we do not see the world as it is, we see it according

Introduction

to who we are. To more fully understand your children, you need to appreciate that they came into the world as different individuals and observers as well. Consequently, a key theme right throughout this book is to parent each child according to whom they are, not according to who you are.

It is not so long ago that if you had a preference to be left handed you were forced to use your right hand, which for some had negative long term consequences. We now know there is a physiological difference. We now know that children are born with different wiring in their brains. This equates to different preferences for making sense of the world. We will explain this in greater depth throughout the book, but we wish to emphasise that we must listen to and observe our children to try to understand who they are and give them the confidence to be who they are.

As we go through each chapter we hope to demonstrate to you that understanding yourself and each child is a critical factor to having positive relationships. If you remain consciously in an inquiring mind, and listen to each individual, you will find different ways of interacting. In this book you will learn about new distinctions so you can observe the world of parenting differently. You will better understand yourself, the relationships you have, and how you might be as a parent. We encourage you to be active learners and to be open to possibilities.

As parents, you have the most important role in the world. We invite you to read this book in a mood of curiosity and wonder, remaining open to investigation and possibilities. We invite you to consciously examine some of the ideas you hold about parenting; with awareness comes the ability to do things differently. You will learn how to manage problems that arise, confident that you know your child and have the skills to respond in the most appropriate way. A happier family is one that recognises and respects one another's differences. We believe children who are accepted for who they are will grow to be adults with well developed social and emotional skills. They will have the power to make the world a happier place.

In writing this book we call on knowledge and skills we collectively have from the fields of psychology, ontology, education, from being parents, and for Graeme, a grandparent. This includes our reflections on the mistakes we assess we have made and what we have learnt as a result.

CHAPTER 2: LEARNING TO LEARN

We claim there is no such thing as a parenting expert, and parenting is (thankfully) continually evolving. The rate of change in everything we do seems to be getting faster, and parenting is no exception. This is demonstrated so aptly by Robin Grille in his book, *Parenting for a Peaceful World*, where, in the first part of his book, he takes the reader through the appalling history of the way we have treated children, given the observers we are today.

There are so many inputs that influence the unique ways we parent our children. These inputs include books, magazines, child health professionals, cultural practices, social customs, religious beliefs, our own personalities – self-confidence, self-esteem, stress and, our own individual preferences for how we make sense of the world. One of the most powerful influences is how we were parented, which is why Chapter 5 examines the Childhood Origins of Parenting. We claim that the better you understand yourself, and the closer you can get to and listen to your child, the more you will be able to trust yourself and your own intuition about parenting decisions, and develop your own unique parenting style and way of being.

The philosopher, John R. Searle, in an interview with Bill Mayers made this point very clear. He said:

"You can teach people to get to the point where they can teach themselves. I don't think I can teach my students how to do philosophy, but I certainly put their noses in it, and tell them where they're making mistakes, so that eventually they can teach themselves. The distressing thing about this is when they get really good, they start refuting me. This is very annoying, but officially at least, I have to recognise the desirability of that. When they can get to the point where they can respect their teacher, or respect the books I ask them to read, and nonetheless point out what seem to them to be inadequacies, then I know we're on the right track."[1]

We want to discuss the issue of learning and not learning. There are several areas in our lives where we develop a resistance to learning and we continue to perform ineffective action. We have come to notice that one of these areas is parenting, which is understandable as there is so much unsolicited advice and criticism given to parents. We find that most of the resistance to learning comes from two basic assessments people make when confronted with new opportunities to learn.

The first is that people often don't see what is new as new, or they don't see what else there is to learn about a topic. A common reaction we have listened to when declaring writing a book about parenting is amusement and, "What could you possibly write about that topic that

[1] Echeverria, Rafael., Ph.D., The Newfield Group, paper, *Learning to Learn*, 1991

has not been written already." There is a major problem with this; if we don't test our assumptions, we may miss something new. We must start with a willingness to accept that we may not know all there is to know, or a willingness to question our existing knowledge, test our assumptions and be open to the possibility that we don't hold the truth about something (or maybe anything!), and that we may learn something new.

It is wiser to assume we do not know than to assume we do. A Chilean biologist, Humberto Maturana, sees human beings as both conserving (maintaining our coherence about the world) and expanding (open to change), which is all about balance. Unless we let go of our current way of thinking about parenting it is difficult to open up to and acknowledge what might be a new way of thinking and being.

Children are very good at learning as they are far less concerned with being conservative about what they know. They also have less learning and fewer assumptions that they need to defend. On the other hand parents may say, "This is all too hard, I can't learn this." This may stem back to lack of self-confidence, and this lack of self-confidence could well come from their own experiences of being parented. Maybe one of their parents, in a moment of stress and/or frustration, said to them, "You are so dumb." Some of this goes right through to the subconscious and sticks! This lack of self-confidence is not only an assessment that people hold about themselves, but also an emotional state. Emotional states are a disposition, or a lack of disposition, for action. Some common emotional states in the domain of parenting are: anxiety, indignation and anger, versus curiosity and wonder.

In Alison's experience, when young children are learning to read, they happily invent a story from the pictures in a book. As early writers, they make squiggles on the paper, write some letters they may know or words they know, then read what they have written (even though to others it's unreadable). It saddens us to see young children unwilling to try to read or write because they have seen what other children can do, or they've been told by older children, often siblings, that they are dumb. Suddenly, what started as wonderful exploration becomes a task that is too hard; this quickly leads to frustration for the child and the parents.

Sometimes the enemies of learning may show up when we look at learning about external things versus learning things about us and our way of being. We find in our coaching that most people claim they are very open to learning, but this is about 'it', be it parenting or leadership or formal qualifications. Many are not open to learning about themselves and how they might learn to be a different observer of the world, to have a different way of being in the world, to behave differently. Many people read and learn about parenting but this often does not translate into 'doing' parenting differently. A common response we listen to are variations of, "This is the way I am." It is okay to be a learner, to say, "I don't know at this moment." It is okay to declare yourself a learner, have a go and maybe get it wrong. Learning may result!

What do we mean when we talk about different observers? As mentioned previously, we claim we do not see the world as it is, we see it as we are. Furthermore we claim we do not hold the truth about something, rather we hold what shows up for us as the truth. Many family arguments arise because two people are holding the truth about some issue. Many times this is about two people coming together as parents and each claiming to know the correct way to parent a child. When someone feels that they hold the truth about something, they have the motivation to have the other comply with their interpretation of the truth. See also Chapter 4 where we discuss competitive thinking.

When this happens we also get ourselves into an inappropriate mood for any further conversation. We lock ourselves into being defensive. If we could allow ourselves to be open to the possibility that our assumptions may be incorrect, and our answers may be incorrect, and move into a different emotional space, then we can have a different conversation.

When we use the term conversation, we use this to mean any form of communication we can have, and through all the different mediums that we can have conversations. We hope that through reading this book we are having a conversation with you, the reader. If we refer to the Chambers 20th Century Dictionary for the Latin derivation of conversation where we find that 'conversarie' means to turn about, 'versarie' is to keep turning and 'vertere' is to turn. So, hopefully, through our conversations we are able to move together.

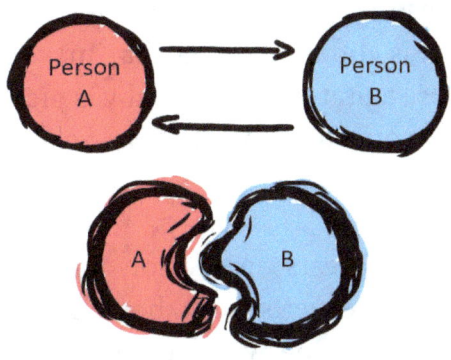

We can take this notion of different observers one more step when it comes to learning how to learn. Imagine the situation where your baby is crying and no matter what you do it does not help, and your baby is becoming more and more agitated. Then along comes someone else who cuddles and gently rocks the baby, perhaps strokes the back of his hand and he falls asleep as if by magic. What happened? Well, maybe the other person came in as a different observer of the situation, saw you were getting more anxious and agitated and listened to the baby wanting to be held, but not by someone who is anxious and agitated.

So how does the notion of different observers help you, apart from getting your baby to sleep? We have an interpretation adopted from Chris Argyris and Echeverria that, in a situation such as this, you were caught up in what Echeverria has termed 'first order learning'. You tried this and it either works or doesn't work. First order learning works well a lot of the time. Baby cries and baby is fed and baby sleeps. That is first order learning. The situation above requires us to step out of the situation and ask ourselves how we are observing this in the first instance. How might we observe this differently? Ah ha, maybe I am getting more and more agitated and the baby is picking up on this. What if I take some deep breaths and relax and then smile at my baby?

> A couple of years ago Alison had a group of educational 'experts' visit her classroom on a regular basis. One woman commented that it was wonderful, and just what a Prep classroom

should be like, while another said that it was extremely noisy and they were a group of very naughty children. Those two people were different observers.

An interpretation that we find very relevant to learning to learn is the four domains of learning. They are as follows:

1. **Not know what we don't know (Unconscious Incompetence)**

   Aggressive parents teach children to be aggressive. The parents and then the children don't even know that they don't know a better way. In our coaching we find that aggression is so transparent to many clients that they genuinely believe that they are not being aggressive. Often it comes as quite a shock to them when they are provided with evidence that this is so. Small children have a whole world of what it is they don't know they don't know. For example, they don't know that they don't know about geography or mathematics. New born babies don't know about time or that there is a future. How could they? They don't know about language that provides such distinctions.

2. **Knowing we don't know (Conscious Incompetence)**

   We can create breakdowns by giving grounded feedback such that parents come to realise that they might be operating from a particular style. In using the Human Synergistics 360 degree feedback instrument known as the Life Styles Inventory (LSI) we have people come to see how they have learnt to be, how they think before they act. We discuss the Human Synergistics work and the LSI more in Chapter 5. For example, we know we don't know what it is really like to be raised and live in a foreign country. We do know we do not know. Often we take this one step further; when people come to our country from a foreign culture, we label them as wrong, incompetent and ignorant. When Alison was teaching, the mother of an Asian boy used to come to school each lunch time to feed her son, who was in his first year of school. There was a lot of discussion amongst the teachers about this, and she was judged by most as being wrong. Alison had lived in Singapore for two years and observed many Asian parents feeding their children for much longer than most parents here do. Are they wrong, or do they have different practices?

We find in our coaching and in our own way of being, that it is freeing to declare ourselves ignorant and to be learners. Many people become anxious and embarrassed to admit they don't know. We are not, and never will be, all knowing beings! A major resistance to learning as adults is a reluctance to be beginners. As new parents, declare yourselves beginners and listen to your baby, your instincts and other sources of information and try to be in a mood of wonder and curiosity.

So with children, at least initially, they don't know they don't know and then they know they don't know. We advocate the more rich and varied the environment is for children, the more they have the opportunity to learn. For example, children who are given the opportunity, on some occasions, to go to restaurants, learn what they don't know about behaviour in restaurants and have the opportunity to practise appropriate behaviour.

Generally speaking we observe there are two broad philosophies that parents adopt, at least in our western cultures. One is where the world of the parents rotates almost entirely around the child or children, which often has a limiting impact on the exposure of children to a rich environment, including who is called upon to mind them and assist with parenting. The other philosophy is where the parents adopt an attitude that the children fit in with them. This philosophy has the children exposed to more carers, and a richer environment when they go out with parents and children who know what is expected under various circumstances. It is okay for babies and toddlers to sometimes experience night life outside of the home; to experience city lights, the stars and the moon. Of course, both of these philosophies have extremes which can become detrimental to the welfare of the children. We can have children with a restricted environment and children who are dragged everywhere. Both may have limited opportunity for the children to have time to do what they want to do. We believe the best teachers are your children. Listen to them and they will tell you when they are tired or have had enough.

3. **Knowing we know (Conscious Competence)**

When you decide you are going to do something in a different, new or more effective way, you begin practising doing it this way. It requires you to consciously practise doing it this way. What joy it brings to us all when we witness a baby take the first step! For young children this can take a lot of time and patience and you may be calling on the child to practise far more than you might realise. Listen to your child and if the timing is right, use some gentle encouragement and praise with any behaviour which is in any way inclined to be in the direction you are aiming for.

4. **Transparency (Unconscious Competence – Unconscious Incompetence)**

After you have been practising doing this new competence it becomes transparent. You don't think about walking or talking most of the time, you just do it. Following on from those first steps that baby took, there is the odd tumble, but very quickly the walking becomes transparent to the toddler. One of the wonderful things is that, as we master certain learning, it is transferred into our unconscious and this frees us up to consciously learn new things. However, with parenting, we often unconsciously do what we do, given our upbringing – our own unique ways of being parented by our parents. This is what we mean by unconscious incompetence. In times of frustration and/or stress, you might find yourself being aggressive and yelling at your children because that is what your parent(s) did. You might find yourself smacking your child because that is what your parent(s) did. You might even hear yourself sounding like your mother or father. You may even defend your actions by saying, "It didn't hurt me" – but did it?

Some of our fondest memories influence our parenting style, but so do our most unpleasant memories. Some of the unpleasant memories influence us to do the same when we are angry, and some of our unpleasant memories influence us to over compensate. For example, if we were raised by autocratic aggressive defensive parents, we may gravitate to being very passive defensive, and our children go unchecked.

Our invitation in this book is to continually create a breakdown of this transparent way of being, so that you continue to be investigative, observe yourself, to question and to learn to refine your parenting.

In conclusion:

- Our invitation is for you to read the remainder of what this book has to offer in a mood of curiosity and wonder.

- Start by wondering – who are these little people we call children? How can we connect with them and try to understand who they are? This way we might be able to nurture what they have come into the world with, rather than forcing them to be someone they are not.

- Work on understanding yourself, your personal and cultural history and its impact on who you are, your relationships and how you might be as a parent.

- Work to better understand your children. The closer you can get to, and listen to your child, the more you will be able to trust yourself and your own intuition about parenting decisions and to investigate and develop your own unique parenting style, and way of being.

- Connect with your inner wisdom and intuition, and listen to your own and your baby/child's needs.

- Be active learners; be open to investigation, possibilities and to being different as a parent. Start with a willingness to accept that you may not know and a willingness to question your existing knowledge, test your assumptions and be open to the possibility that you don't hold the truth about something, and that you may learn something new.

- Observe how you are observing and maybe observe things differently. Understand there are things in the world you don't even know you don't know. This is especially important in understanding and listening to babies and young children. Understand there are things you know you don't know, but that it is okay to declare yourself a learner. When learning new things it is a conscious thing and will require patience and practise. Once you have mastered something it becomes transparent, you put it into the subconscious which then allows you to learn other new things.

- Finally this is not about right or wrong, good or bad, but an invitation for you to go on a journey to becoming a new way of being as a parent.

CHAPTER 3: LISTENING

As you come to this chapter on listening you are most likely engaging in some private self-talk or thinking about this topic. We hope that you might be in a mood of curiosity, wondering what we might be about to say. We claim that listening to your baby and to children is a critical skill. We repeat we are all different observers of the world, and we do not see the world as it is – we see it according to how we are. To more fully understand your children, you need to appreciate that they came into the world as different observers as well. Research now shows that babies do not come into the world with a clean slate. As we said in Chapter 1, and we repeat here because we consider it so important, children are all uniquely different. We all know this, yet sometimes we behave as if this is not true. We think our children should be the way we think they should be. Consequently, a key theme right throughout this book is to parent each child according to whom they are, not according to how you or others think they should be. This is a critical factor to having happier children and then happier adults. To do this we must listen and be investigative, with as many distinctions as we can, to better understand each child. Every child is special and they all have special needs. In Chapter 6 we will discuss how to balance the child's special needs with your own and others' needs.

Some of you may be thinking that there are times when maybe you could have listened more effectively, or that you were not listening at all. Maybe there is room for you to improve on your listening. If so then we believe we can help you. Some of you might be thinking, "What is there to say about listening that I have not already read?" or "I have read all about active listening back in the 70's and 80's." Others of you may be thinking, "Here they go again, making the simple complex." Whatever self-talk or thinking that you are listening to as you begin to read this chapter, and other chapters of this book for that matter, will impact on how you listen to the content of what we have to say. This is why we claim that listening comes before speaking. Before we expand on this claim we want to make the distinction between listening and hearing.

Listening and Hearing

Hearing is something we can measure. We have hearing tests to establish the health of our hearing. When we are put in a sound proof booth for our hearing test, until there is a sound we cannot hear anything. There are no vibrations on our eardrums. When we are watching a film we hear music and voices and all sorts of other sounds. When there are no sounds we can't hear anything but we claim that you can listen to silence. When watching a drama unfold in a film we are listening to all kinds of sounds including music to build up our emotions and expectations of the unfolding drama. Then there is silence right at the very moment when we expect something dramatic to happen. At this point it is the silence that we are listening to that has us on the edge of our seats. But at this moment we can't hear anything, at least from the film, unless the cat jumps on the tin roof at this precise moment!

What is Listening?

To define listening we have a simple formula:

Listening = Five Senses + Interpretation.

We originally would have it that listening = hearing + interpretation, until one day we thought about a friend of ours who works with the hearing impaired, and we came to the conclusion that although some of the hearing impaired cannot hear anything they can still listen. With sign language the hearing impaired can listen through seeing. A gentle hand on your shoulder can also be 'listened to' in many ways, from a message of caring or love to, "Could I please move past you?"

The Five Senses

If we take this interpretation further, we claim that we do use all five senses in our listening. If you think of occasions when you 'heard' what someone was saying but somehow you didn't believe them, it may have been your other senses that came into play. What you saw when they were speaking may have you listen to something else – body language. When watching TV interviews, what we hear and see impacts on our listening. When someone gently lays a hand on us, what is being said and what we observe will impact on what we listen to. So how does taste and smell impact on what we listen to? If the director of a company was to address angry neighbours to claim that the air was clean, they will be listening to something else when the smell suggests otherwise. If we visit a winery that claims to make beautiful wines and we taste a wine and find the bouquet offensive and the taste unpleasant, our listening will be somewhat different from the words we 'hear' from the winemaker. These are some obvious examples. However, the five senses often play a key role in subtle ways. Our listening can be impacted upon if someone is wearing nice perfume or aftershave. If someone is overpowering with perfume or has bad body odour, this can impact on our listening. Perhaps you can recall a time when you were in a hot, stuffy room trying to listen to the presenter, you cannot see the board or screen, and to top it off you are desperate to visit the bathroom. In this sort of situation you will be hearing but not listening and little of what the presenter says will be remembered. When your baby cries, you may check if she needs her nappy changed, or is hungry, in pain or tired. As a parent of a baby you already use your five senses to interpret your baby's cry.

But what about when we are listening to our inner thoughts, our 'private speak' or self-talk, our internal chatter, even our intuition? Well, there are a number of things to consider here. We acquire language and memories through our senses. Our brain does not make the distinction between real and imagined memories, between memory of real experiences and memories of those vivid dreams. If you think of the brain as having been programmed, when we listen to that internal conversation it is the same neurons that are being fired as when we listen to someone else speak. This applies not only to listening to and being mindful of our internal or private speak, but to all of the senses. You can remember the warm feeling of the sun on your back, you can remember seeing and smelling the sea and you can remember the taste and smell of your favourite meal. Had you not ever experienced any of these through your five senses you could not reflect on the experiences. To the best of our knowledge no other animals engage in self-talk to the degree that we do. They do not have the same capacity for language nor the ability to program their brain in the way we do.

Interpretation

The interpretation we apply to our listening comes from our history of personal experiences, concerns, emotions, intuition and our culture, to mention just a few. Now that we have this interpretation about listening and different cultures we are significantly more careful with our speaking. We try to ensure listening that is more in line with our speaking. We consciously aim to design our speaking for the listener in the hope that we will be more accurately listened to. If we mention a 'sleepover' in Australia this means a stay overnight at a friend's place. In some other cultures this can have very different meanings. With your experiences certain moods and emotions may also show up. I have very fond memories of travelling on country trains with my family to visit relatives. Some people may have had bad experiences on trains so their interpretations when they think about trains may be different.

In this sketch, what is being listened to?

We often use a poem called *In the Village* by Andrew Oerke as an exercise in listening. On one occasion when I read the poem out to a group and then inquired of people where the village was for them, one lady replied, "In Mount Waverley." I was surprised, as I live in Mount Waverley and when I said so she replied, "Well, obviously you don't do the shopping!" Mount Waverley has what is known as The Mount Waverley Village Shopping Centre. The responses are usually governed by life experiences, recent or otherwise. Some recall villages in their travels, others recall recent films or books they have read.

Intuition

We do not want to get into a debate about what intuition is, or whether intuition exists or not, nor where it comes from. For the purposes of this book let's just assume that it does exist. When we listen to our self-talk, often buried in amongst it are some ideas or thoughts that we may have no clue as to their origin. Many call it their 'gut feeling'. Listening to this is also critical in the role of parenting. Have you ever had a thought but dismissed it, only to find out later it was very relevant?

Parenting can be very demanding and stressful along with everything else in life that we believe we have to do. The key to effective parenting is to take care of you. We will discuss this in depth in Chapter 5. If you interrupt your 'busyness' and take time out to relax, not only will it help your body, but often you will find that your intuition will speak to you. Great benefits can be gained by just closing your eyes and focussing on your breathing for five breaths, or lying down and meditating/relaxing for ten minutes or so. Maybe next time your baby is crying for no apparent reason, close your eyes momentarily, focus on your breathing and relax. Listen to your intuition, then open your eyes and look into your baby's eyes and see what shows up for you both.

The Three 'A's' of Listening

So what do we mean when we claim that listening comes before speaking? Before you picked up this book you looked at it, wondered about the content, the author, its appearance and, given what you already know about the topic, the author, ontology, whatever, it all impacts on your listening before you read it. At the start of this and other chapters we have talked about what you might already be thinking. This is because before anyone speaks we are:

1. **Already listening**

    In varying degrees some of it is positive, some is negative, all however impacts on how well we do or don't listen. Our 'already listening' impacts on what authority we give the speaker. If we have had previous experiences with the person who is about to speak to us, we will have certain assessments about them, positive or negative. We will be keen to listen or not listen depending on previous experiences. If we have never met the person we may be unwillingly, in the short term at least, to give them any authority; they may be representing a group that we have reservations about. It may be our own biases and prejudices that feed our already listening. So what was your 'already listening' about us when you first picked up this book? Was it based upon what you read about us or on what you already know about us? What is your 'already listening' when you understand that Alison is a mother of two children and has been a primary school teacher for over twenty years? What is your 'already listening' when you understand that Graeme has three boys and currently four grandchildren, and is a qualified psychologist? What is your 'already listening' when you understand that both of us are trained practicing ontological coaches?

One trap for parents is to label a baby, such as feisty, fussy or difficult. The trap is that it potentially becomes a self-fulfilling prophecy and can impact on your (already) listening to your baby's crying. "Oh, here we go again; he is such a feisty baby", or "She is such a difficult baby." So then you have an explanation and so you don't need to listen anymore to what the crying is about – "It's just her being difficult!" This is also why we encourage you to be very careful about labelling your child, not only by you, but by others. Ask yourself – Is this label useful or potentially harmful? Many of these labels stay with the child throughout their life. Think of how you think and act with children who you have been told are 'uncontrollable', or who have a certain diagnosed disorder.

What is your baby really trying to tell you? Based on what we know, we must consider the real possibility there is no such thing as an inherently difficult baby. You, as parents, may have difficulty listening and understanding your baby's needs, particularly if you feel unsupported yourselves, or if your baby has gone through a stressful time in the womb, at birth or soon after. The important thing here is to listen, investigate and to validate what your baby is feeling and respond with love, sensitivity and tenderness.

2. **Always listening**

Often you will hear people say, "You're not listening." We don't believe you can say this, because in our interpretation you are always listening. You may not be listening to the speaker but you will be listening to something, even if it is your own internal chatter. You may not be listening to the baby or child but listening to, "I wish he would be quiet so I can watch TV", or, "I wish she would be quiet so I can read my book." You might be hearing the words but not listening to the speaker. You might be hearing the crying but not listening to the crying. However, in our interpretation you are always listening to something. As parents, it is your key responsibility to listen carefully to your babies and children, combined with your own intuition and internal chatter.

3. **Automatic listening**

What we listen to is automatic. We simply listen to what we listen to. "Ah, here we go again. He is such a demanding baby!" We don't stop and ask ourselves before we listen, "How am I going to listen to this?"

We simply listen to what we listen to given who we are. We can, however, ask ourselves, "How am I listening to this and how might I listen to it differently?" Of course, different circumstances and contexts will impact on what we listen to at any point in time. How many times have you been listening to someone in a crowded room when suddenly you pick up on someone over the other side of the room who says your name in their conversation? It is like we are programmed to pick up on it. You were not consciously listening to other people in the room but you do automatically listen to it at that moment. Then you probably listen to, "What are they saying about me?"

Some Claims about Listening

1. Listening comes before speaking as we have spoken about above.

2. Listening is a process we actively engage in – it is an active process.

3. When we speak it is our intention that we will be listened to in the way that we want. We often find it upsetting when we feel we are not being listened to. How does your baby or child feel when they are not being listened to? Sometimes we speak to listen to ourselves. I often hear people apparently talking to themselves, or are they just thinking aloud? Sometimes, given that I am within earshot, I wonder if I am supposed to be listening. So when you speak to your children, think carefully about how you speak

to them to ensure they will be listening to you and not something else.

4. When we are listened to, it provides an opportunity to validate our speaking.

5. Finally, as I am sure we all know, speaking by no means ensures listening or even hearing.

Effective Listening

Given what we have already covered, it is a miracle that we ever get our interpretation of the listening to be close to the intentions by the speaker. We can never be absolutely certain that what we intended to say is what is listened to by others! We assume that the other person has listened to exactly what we meant, far, far too often. Most of us know only too well the importance of having the listener tell us what they listen to us saying, i.e. summarizing. How many of us can honestly say we request this often enough? I can't! So how can we move towards more effective listening?

When listening, also consider where this person is speaking from. How might they experience the world differently from you? Consider gender, race, culture, history, historical discourse (stories), historical ways of coping, history of personal experiences, concerns and emotions, preferences and prejudices. In coaching and counselling we must consider all this in order to be able to listen to what is being said. We are not suggesting that parents and carers have to be coaches and counsellors with all the knowledge, skills and attributes of full time professional coaches and counsellors. We are saying, however, that good childcare and parenting does involve as much as is possible of the knowledge, skills and attributes of being good coaches and counsellors. Much of our coaching comes about because children and/or partners have not been listened to effectively.

We would like to offer you some examples to clarify what we mean here, to ensure as much clarity for you as listeners of what we have to say. Let us start with gender as an example.

For us males of the species, I find it useful to assume we have no idea what it is like to be a woman. So part of my listening is, what is it like to be a woman? I have no idea what it is like to be Alison and the reverse applies. Louann Brizendine in her book, *The Female Brain*, provides compelling evidence and wonderful insights into the differences between the female brain and the male brain. I have no idea what it is like to be a mother, only what being a father is to me.

We could do well to assume we don't know what it is like to be a baby, your baby. In Chapter 5, we will explore with you the distinctions associated with how we all prefer to make sense of the world in different ways, such as Myers Briggs Type Indicator (MBTI). An example using the MBTI preferences is that we might have two babies – one with an Introvert preference, and one with an Extrovert preference. Babies with a tendency towards Introversion who may not be tired when it is time for bed will more than likely be happy to be put to bed as they are happy with their own company. The baby with the tendency towards Extroversion may be tired when it is time for bed, but will more than likely cry when put to bed, as she wants to continue to be around people. Often this is a baby who stops as soon as we go into the room and cries again when we leave them.

We only know how we see the world; we can only wonder how you see it.

Whenever someone speaks they are always speaking from some concern. When I first heard Julio Olalla make this claim during a conference in San Francisco I initially didn't believe him. As I reflected more on this I came to believe maybe this is so. My first thoughts were that I am one of those people who just babble on but then I thought about everything I say and I have to admit it is always from some concern. Even when I say "Hi" to you every time I pass you in the passageway, it is out of concern for our relationship. I now listen more intently to what the concerns might be when someone is speaking to me. Sometimes, especially in coaching sessions, I might ask why they are telling me this. In a mood of wonder, when you are unsure what the concern of the speaker is, you might inquire as to what is the concern and/or why they are telling you this.

Listening to your baby

So whenever your baby cries, our interpretation is that the baby cries from some concern, and as crying is the only major form of communication, it is possible he may simply want to be listened to. There is often opportunity to listen more carefully, maybe with some more distinctions, to the different cries from babies, ranging from extremely agitated to just being noisy. When listening to them, also be mindful of what is happening around you and to yourself and how you might be contributing.

Listening to your child

As children learn to use language, their ability to verbalise their needs and wants increases. But how do we listen to, and interpret, what our child is trying to tell us? The key to meeting the needs of a child is something we like to call 'relaxed responsiveness'.

Listening requires:

- Time (can be negotiated): The time to listen may be when the child has calmed down, or when you have time to listen.
- An acceptance of your child's feelings.
- A trust in the child's capacity to handle his feelings and solve problems.
- Your ability to accept and not fear negative emotions.
- Your recognition of your child as a unique human being.
- When you are listening to a child, it may help to ask yourself, "Who owns the problem?" Let your child own the problem if it is her problem (i.e. not directly affecting you). Allow her to own the problem and find the solution.

Listening to your Teenager

When we are listening to our children and wondering who they are and what it might be like to be them, it is also helpful to consider yourself and the role you are currently playing as a parent. As we grow older, (parents and children!) it is important to remember just that. When you have a conversation with your son or daughter today, you and your son or daughter are not the same people as yesterday. Both have expanded, matured or changed somewhat. It is like when you return to a spot at the river, you are not the same person and it's not the same river. The shift might be subtle but everything keeps changing.

Often as parents we don't notice these changes until our children become teenagers and start pushing back more powerfully. They want to assume more authority and to lessen your authority as parents. We find it helps with your listening to understand what is happening and to gradually alter your relationship more towards being a confidant and close friend. You can begin to notice and listen to the early signs of a young adult starting to emerge.

One of the issues we help people with, both parents and young adults, is when to let go of the parent/child relationship and move towards interacting as adults. As a general rule we say that by the mid twenties healthy relationships and conversations should be as adult to adult. Some of you may be interacting with your children as children after that time and that can have a detrimental effect on you as parents as well as your dependants. It can result in over protected dependants or overly dependent dependants. Some of you may be thinking that you should cease the parenting before that. Well there is a growing body of research based evidence that young people, both males and females, are not hard wired to think of the consequences of their actions until after they are 25 years old! To us as parents and grandparents this is a bit disconcerting. We can keep reminding our young adults to be responsible, but after that, relinquish your role as parents and become close friends and confidants.

The Five Speech Acts and Listening

In our listening, things show up differently when we have certain distinctions. We subscribe to the distinction that there are five speech acts and understanding these enhances our listening and our speaking. The five speech acts are:

1. Assertions
2. Declarations (including Assessments)
3. Requests
4. Offers
5. Promises (Commitments)

We can become much more competent with our listening when we listen for the distinctions between the five speech acts.

1. **Assertions**

    True assertions are facts, but there are also pending and false assertions. Your baby may be so many months old, be a certain weight, be so long etc., all of which can be measured. When measured we can then say they are true or false. But what if a health professional says your baby will be a certain weight when he/she is six months old? This is what we would call a pending assertion.

2. **Declarations (including Assessments)**

    Declarations come in many forms. We have formal declarations such as, "I declare you husband and wife", or less formal declarations such as, "I am going shopping." Some people, especially children, often make declarations and expect others to take some action as if it was a request. "I am hungry", or "I am thirsty." Their concern is evident and often what follows is an offer by the listener. "Would you like a ...?" However, we don't need to take any action from a declaration.

Assessments are also declarations. When you say your baby is feisty, fussy or difficult these are assessments, although you may well hold them as facts (Assertions). If we are not careful we can listen to assessments as though they are assertions. "She is a shy child" sounds like a true assertion (a fact); however, with careful listening you will listen to it as an assessment. This can open up opportunities which listening to it as an assertion does not. Assessments are made in the moment and we base them on the past, to predict the future. If we hold them for what they are, just assessments that we hold as the observers we are, then they may well not predict the future. One of the very transparent problems with declarations (especially assessments), is that we think we are describing things and overlook that in doing so we are also creating the future. Hence the caution re 'labelling'! Is a label helpful or damaging?

3. **Requests**

Many parents are reluctant to make requests and this then is adopted by children. As a result many will make declarations as mentioned above. A reluctance to make requests is a fear that we will be rejected as a person. But a knockback to a request is simply that; our request was declined at the time, which does not mean every request we ever make will be denied, or that the other person is rejecting who we are.

If you are feeling overwhelmed or stressed with the demands of being parents, then it is useful to realize there is a whole network of help out there just waiting to be tapped into.

4. **Offers**

As mentioned above, when a child declares, "I am hungry", we typically jump into making an offer. We claim that in these situations, children could be encouraged to make effective requests. When we listen to our life partner, sons and daughters, friends or neighbours getting overwhelmed or stressed with parenting, we could make offers.

5. **Promises**

When requests or offers are made and accepted then we say you have a promise or commitment. When an offer is made, the responsibility for the action is with the speaker. When a commitment or promise is made, the associated action is with the person who accepted the request or with the person who made the offer.

All very obvious you say. We agree. We see it as making you aware of the obvious, or making the apparent obvious. So why do we do this? We offer to you that most of our conversations are so transparent we do not see the many pitfalls. We will now discuss some of the possible consequences of these actions and what possibilities could be opened or closed. We will discuss requests, offers and promises in greater depth later.

Listening and Emotions

Moods and emotions play a big part in how well we listen. This is why, as parents, we must work at managing our moods and emotions. We can hardly be responsible for the moods and emotions we find ourselves in, however we can be mindful and choose to change those moods and emotions. We will talk more about managing moods and emotions in Chapter 4.

It is difficult not to become angry and defensive when faced with disagreements, challenges and difficulties. Instead of being defensive, try listening to what is being said in a mood of curiosity and wonder. Put your own ego off to the side and listen carefully. Check your listening with what is being said. You may not be listening to the message in the way it is intended. Even if you are receiving a clear message, then listen for the concerns, the evidence to support the assertions, and the grounding to support the assessments. What is this person telling you about yourself and/or your family and what are they telling you about themselves? When self-esteem is healthy and there is power within us, it becomes much easier to be less defensive and to be in a positive mood of wonder and curiosity and to learn. Remember, we are all different observers of the world.

An appropriate conversation in an inappropriate mood is, in our interpretation, an inappropriate conversation. This becomes more important as your children get older. If it is your mood then take steps to change it. If the other person is very emotional, acknowledge their emotions and check to see if you should continue now or maybe organize a time to have the conversation later.

Remember that your mood could well be the difference between you being assertive and you being seen as aggressive, bullying and intimidating. Sure, when you turn the heat up things really get going, but what are the long-term consequences?

Stephen Covey in his book, *Seven Habits of Highly Effective People*, speaks to one habit being to 'Seek First to Understand and Then Be Understood'. We have seen too many examples where parents, childcare professionals and teachers' already listening, emotions, biases and judgments have had them go straight to being understood without effectively listening. The message and/or concerns by the speaker and the associated opportunities are lost, and the relationship possibly further damaged. Often the result is also damage to the person's self-esteem and self-confidence, and a reluctance to engage in further conversations.

Mastering awareness involves being mindful of everything that is going on around and for us, our already listening, our stories and assessments (much of which equates to our prejudices and biases), and of course, being aware of our moods and emotions. In these situations, if we wish to be truly effective as parents, we must rise above ourselves and question how we are, and how we are observing. Only then do we have the opportunity to ask ourselves how we could observe things differently. Mastering awareness also has to do with the environment you are in at any moment. All this is very relevant to how we listen to our babies and children.

Some children are more persistent about getting the message across than others. One student in Alison's class who came from a non-English speaking background was quite happy to shrug her shoulders when she didn't understand, and would show Alison what she wanted. Another child became upset when Alison couldn't understand what he was saying, and withdrew. Alison, as a teacher, often said or read something to the students that she assumed they would understand, but when she checked in with them, realized they had a different interpretation. Recently, they were talking about being safe in the sun and had watched a YouTube clip about 'Slip, Slop, Slap, Seek and Slide'. The word 'slide' in this context refers to sliding on some sunglasses, but very few of the students understood this; as far as they were concerned, slide is a piece of playground equipment.

Too many verbal instructions can also be very difficult for many children to listen to. Some children have difficulty processing verbal instructions, and something like, "Pack up you toys, wash your hands, then come and have dinner", may be too much to process. Only the last, "Come and have dinner", may have been remembered.

Teenagers: Your teenager has asked your permission to attend a party. After some investigation, you find this party will not be well supervised and, for a number of reasons, you do not want your teenager to go. You explain to your teenager why you are not going to let them go, and this is not well received. Their interpretation of your reasons may sound something like this: "You never let me do anything. Everyone else is allowed to go. You don't you trust me.", and so on.

Like all the stages of life, your teenager needs your empathy, understanding, help with managing emotions and importantly, your trust.

In conclusion:

- Listen, listen, listen and then listen!!! Listen, at least as much as you can, in a mood of curiosity and wonder – and be investigative!

Listening

- Know that we listen with all of our senses.

- Be mindful of the many factors that influence how we interpret what we hear.

- Remember that I only know how I see the world; I can only wonder how you see it.

CHAPTER 4: MOODS AND EMOTIONS

Our moods and emotions are central to the role of parenting and to the long term wellbeing of our children. Moods and emotions are also critical to having more peaceful and happy children and a more peaceful and happy world.

What are moods and emotions?

Emotions are triggered as a result of becoming aware of some moment in our lives. It might be the beautiful smile of a small baby or an act of kindness by someone. It might be a simple thank you note from a friend. Of course there are also the negative emotions that are triggered when someone says or does something that is not to our liking. Our emotions can also be triggered by music, flora, fauna, scenery, and, dare I say, steam trains, etc. Our individual emotional reactions, given the different observers we are, can also be different. Our emotions are a precursor to some actions, and can get in the way of taking some other actions.

    This morning, while in the coffee shop, I observed a couple of sparrows (small birds) flitting from table to table and chair to chair. They were scrounging for crumbs and they would just sit and look at the occupants of each table. Some people observed the birds with a little fascination, and others reacted negatively towards them and waved them away. In each person, I observed an emotional reaction that predisposed their response. I sat and wondered about the sparrows. I looked at their eyes and they looked back at me and I became aware that I had a story about them – my story, not theirs, obviously. However, my emotional reaction was a mixture of fascination and curiosity.

Moods are different from emotions, although sometimes the distinction seems to be subtle, as it can be difficult to separate one from the other. Unlike emotions, moods are not specific and we normally do not relate them to particular events. As human beings we are always in a mood. No matter where we are or what we are doing, at least when we are awake and conscious, we are in a mood. Not only are we always in a mood, we become our moods.

Some of my clients have said to me their moods have them, not that they have their moods. This is a critical point for having any control over the moods. A person who is in a mood of resentment becomes a resentful person who is predisposed to anger and aggression. When we observe our moods, we are already immersed in them. Just pause for a moment from reading this book and reflect on your mood. For some of you this may be easy, for others you may not be readily able to describe it. It may help to identify what colour comes to mind when you reflect on your mood, and then describe why you chose that particular colour.

If moods have us, does this mean there is nothing we can do about them? Should we be resigned to them? The answer is 'no' to both questions. By observing your mood you can now choose to remain in that mood or to intervene in shaping your mood. You can participate in the design of your mood. If we go back to your reflection on your mood, is this mood working for you or against you in reading this book? Is this mood working for or against you being an effective parent? Do you want your children to develop the same mood(s) as you? What do you need to do if you want to shift this mood? What mood would you like to be in right now? Some of the many options for shifting your mood might be to engage in positive conversations, change your environment, play different music, or call upon your memory of when you were in the preferred mood and replace it. I find 'wonder' to be a fantastic mood when I am reading. The sort of wonder you might experience when doing something enjoyable. I enjoy riding my bike along a rail trail for the first time and wondering what is over the hill or what I will see next.

Moods and emotions are closely linked. If an emotion stays long enough it can become a mood. Some people have, unfortunately, gone through separation and divorce which has been very emotional. These emotions, when left unattended, most often become a mood of resentment, a mood not conducive to positive relationships including with children. What I then observe is that from a mood of resentment come other emotions, such as anger. So not only can emotions become moods, moods can also be the platform from which emotions will spring. The mood of resentment generally has a predisposition for revenge and punishment. When people are in the mood of resentment they are also suffering stress. With the fight or flight of stress you have people who want to fight (aggressive) or run away (passive). The impact of these negative moods is potentially extremely costly not only on relationships and children, but people are more likely to be accident prone.

What is not generally known is that these moods can be shifted. As you may have discovered above, when we become aware of our mood we also become aware of the possibility that we can change it.

My experience this morning with the sparrows was from a mood of wonder and curiosity, so my emotion was one of love and fascination of nature. The mood of others may have been from anxiety or resentment and the birds were a source of annoyance.

Changing Moods and Emotions

Why would we want to change our moods and emotions? For a start, in our interpretation the right conversation in the inappropriate mood is the inappropriate conversation. If you reflect on when you are angry (or sad), you might see that this is the very time you were most in need of understanding. It is these very moments when you are least likely to receive it. When you are angry you do not look very attractive. You are not pleasant to be around and some people may well be afraid of you. A conversation when angry will also have you being aggressive, and this can be enough for you to be seen as bullying and intimidating. We have seen many young people who are frightened to make a decision for fear that if their mother or father does not agree they will experience another angry outburst. Ironically this is a very vicious circle. The young person becomes more and more paralysed and the mother or father becomes more and more angry. Be careful also that you have not become addicted to your anger. Does it make you feel more powerful and as a consequence you get what you want? People do as you say but what are the other (long term) consequences?

We can unconsciously become addicted to a whole range of unhealthy moods and emotions, and can unintentionally reinforce this in our children. Do we get more of what we want when we cry, or sulk, or throw tantrums? If we have bouts of anxiety and depression (which may be related to stress) do we have people run after us more, or can we more readily not do what others expect or request of us? If this has been learnt over a long period of time it can be totally transparent to us and can often prevent us from overcoming it. We can then be locked into anxiety or depression by our story that we suffer from it.

I don't subscribe to the notion that being angry or turning the heat up is necessary to get things really going.

Angry parents create anxiety that is not conducive to long term commitments or motivation and also can impact significantly on children's health and safety. A good parent can be assertive (and even stern) but will have people respect them and willingly follow rather than being dragged or shoved along.

If you approach a challenging situation in a positive, or 'can do' mood, this is the difference between being assertive and aggressive, and can have your children want to go with you rather than comply out of fear.

Moods and emotions are contagious. Unfortunately many seem to 'catch' other people's negative moods more readily than catching positive moods. However, some people have contagious positive moods which are a blessing to have impact on us. Surround yourself with positive people. I once witnessed a policeman interacting with a group of drunken teenagers who had been evicted from a motel. They were angry, swearing and making negative assessments about the motel manager and the policeman. The policeman remained calm and assertive and fobbed off any negative assessments. The net result was that they calmed down. As parents, especially as our children get older, it is critical not to get caught up in their emotional outbursts, as it will decline into a battle with people getting hurt psychologically and potentially physically. In addition, our children then learn this is the way of life and will not learn more effective strategies.

There are many ways for us to shift our own moods and emotions and I will cover some of these. The list is not exhaustive and you may have already developed some good strategies for doing this.

If moods and emotions are precursors for some action and not others, and if some of the actions we would like to take are not possible or feasible, then what can we do? First we must understand that the act of speaking, whether to others or ourselves, is action. So one of the actions available is to linguistically reconstruct what we have observed.

Linguistic Reconstruction has a number of steps, and I shall use an example to explain what I mean by this. When driving home from the airport sometime after midnight, my wife and I witnessed the results of a rather bad car accident. Because I am driven by people not being hurt physically or mentally, I had a quite significant negative emotional reaction. I felt really sad and wanted to help. I quickly assessed that there was nothing I could do as all the emergency services were in attendance along with many bystanders who were probably a hindrance. I said to my wife that it looked like a nasty accident and then I asked what we had planned for tomorrow. As a consequence, I had shifted my emotion somewhat. What I didn't do was to deny my emotions. Please be aware that no effort is made to squash the negative feeling. What we deny or repress returns with greater energy and insistence.

So what are the steps I took?

- Awareness of an incident that stimulated an emotional reaction.
- Awareness of the emotion. Do not fight against it, simply bring calm awareness to noticing it and let it be.

- Awareness of the action I wanted to take as a result of the emotion.
- Decision time. Do I take a certain action (then do it) or not?
- No action, so I need to bring calm non-interfering awareness of the emotion and then do whatever I can to shift the emotion.
- Have a conversation that may help shift the emotions.

What I did was to have a conversation and, in the act of speaking, I acknowledged my emotion and took some action. Further, by having a conversation that also helped to shift the emotion, the intensity lessened significantly. It did not go away completely in the short term but it did not have the same long-term impact – consciously and/or subconsciously – as it could have. If we consider ourselves as wired to be angry or sad, maybe as a result of previous events in our lives, and we observe those moods and emotions in a calm and non-interfering way we are gradually able to de-condition ourselves. The negative emotional energy begins to dissipate.

Conversations impact, both positively and negatively, on our emotions and moods. Many people engage in descriptive conversations – which also include complaining – the greatest percentage of their conversational time. In this type of conversation we think we are merely describing something; however, in the process of describing we are also creating. If I say this is a horrible place to stay, then it will show up for me in the future as being that way, even if the place has changed. The language we use can lock us into not changing our perceptions. In our coaching, we like to engage clients in what are called the 'magic wand' questions. These questions engage people in conversations for possibilities or speculation and it is truly magical how this can have a positive impact on our clients' moods.

Of course the next step is a conversation on how to get there. See Chapters 10 to 12 on types of conversations for greater detail.

Being centred and aligned is an excellent way to shift a negative mood. This is in the domain of the body and is far more than just body language. Being centred is where you stretch your vertebrae which will open up your chest cavity; you straighten your neck and support your head by your neck and shoulders. You can obtain this posture if you imagine a sky hook attached to the top of your head that is pulling you up. Imagine if you don't stretch your vertebrae your feet may not be able to touch the ground. My youngest grandson at twelve months of age is very centred, and my neighbour commented that he walks around as if he owns the place. He is a very happy little guy and readily smiles at anyone.

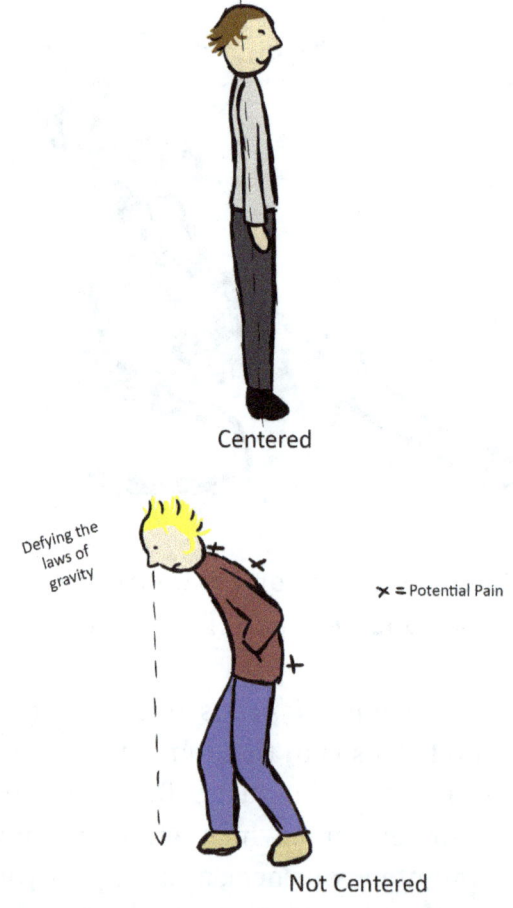

To place your body in a posture of being centred, do the following:

1. Tuck your chin in to elongate your neck and spine
2. Imagine your chest and head are being pulled upward to the sky by an imaginery string
3. Hang your arms at your side in a relaxed manner
4. Align your pelvis under your shoulders
5. Keep your knees slightly bent
6. Place your feet about hip width apart.

Music and Dance are very effective for changing moods. Those of you who are musicians or dancers will already know that there is no stronger stimulant to the emotions. Most people try to find music to suit the mood they are in or don't listen to music because they are not in the mood. A simple little exercise is to select music to suit the mood you want to be in. Try a little movement to this music as well and you may be in for a surprise. For this to work you must first be aware of your mood and the mood you want to be in and be prepared to move towards a different mood. I have fond memories of our family concerts at home. My mum played piano, my dad a thing called a swanny whistle, my sisters played flute, my brother played many instruments including violin and I played drums and we all sang – sort of! There was lots of laughter and great times.

Exercise is very beneficial for shifting to positive moods. Even getting outside for a brief walk can shift things, especially if you are also centred.

Breathing is another entrée into shifting moods. Focus on your breathing. Notice everything about the sensation of breathing in and out; the cool of the air in your nostrils as you breathe in, the warmth of the air as you breathe out and the moment when you are in transition from breathing in and out. Try breathing so deeply that it forces your belly to move out, and do so for five or more breaths. Every time you breathe out relax any muscles that you are holding tense. Repeating this several times a day can have wonderful results.

Changing your environment can also put you in the mood you desire. I am writing in a holiday home at the beach kindly lent to me by a colleague who understands that it creates an environment for me that is conducive to my writing. Stop and look at your home. Does it create the mood you want? How might you change it? You might find a pot plant or some freshly cut flowers could make a big difference. Make sure though that you interrupt your 'busyness' in order to admire them and attend to them. I find my mood is impacted negatively when I go into a home where the poor pot plant is dying or dead through lack of attention and water.

Laughing is excellent for shifting our moods. Children laugh so much but sadly as we grow up we seem to laugh less. Let us try for more laughter in the home and when with the family. What a terrific atmosphere where there is lots of laughter. How great is it when we are served in a shop by someone who seems to be bubbling over with laughter. Customers go away happy and come back for more. A cautionary note however. Please use humour cautiously and be sure it is not at someone else's expense. Humour is seldom innocent. As well as being a catalyst for laughter, some humour can be cruel.

Reflecting on your strengths can effectively overcome negative moods and can help you shift from anxiety to wondering how you will go, or curiosity about how you will perform. I have sometimes felt anxious when playing in the band and the leader turns to me to take a solo. If I stay with anxiety I know it will limit my performance. I quickly remind myself that I can play and just wonder about how the solo will go.

Stress management is a critical practice for managing moods and emotions. As we discuss in Chapter 6, one interpretation of stress that we subscribe to was offered by Yerkes & Dodson. They see we have two kinds of stress. Eustress, or good stress, which works in our favour in everything we do. Dystress is the negative stress, which is what we commonly know as stress. With dystress we have fight or flight and, if extreme, we have freeze. If we are suffering from dystress, we are predisposed to negative emotional outbursts and negative moods. We may become aggressive and intolerant of even the smallest of incidents – we may be looking for a fight. We may become withdrawn and depressed – we want to run away.

To manage stress, we must manage our level of adrenaline. If we don't, our levels of adrenaline will continue to build up in our bodies. Exercise burns it up, and deep relaxation or meditation allows the body to neutralize unspent adrenaline. When we raise our awareness and become mindful of our moods and emotions, they can give us valuable clues as to what our body and mind is up to. We must listen to these clues and intervene accordingly.

Relaxing massages, meditation, yoga, deep relaxation exercises have all been shown to have significant positive impact on our fundamental moods in life. They also reduce our stress levels which makes us less likely to want to fight or flee. Caroline Myss in her book, *Invisible Acts of Power*, tells us that, as a child, the Dalai Lama was as angry as any child and even a bully at times. But after sixty years of meditating and developing compassion, the angry emotions faded away. He doesn't even have to work to suppress any anger; he simply never feels it.

Focus on the present. Eckhart Tolle in his book, *The Power of Now*, speaks of how we become addicted to thinking about the past and the future and the suffering this can bring us. His powerful message is that when we are in the moment of now we are not concerned with either.

Impact of Moods and Emotions

I mentioned above that moods and emotions are contagious. How does this happen? I cannot be sure but my experience tells me it is one of the mysteries of the world. Please don't underestimate its power and its impact on children, other people and animals, on their safety, wellbeing and motivation. I had a client who suffered from anxiety and when he told me he had taken the dog to the vet because it was anxious and running away from home, I inquired if the dog was anxious with his wife. The answer was no! Animals pick up on moods and emotions. So do children. I liken it to fish in the shallows – they zigzag off but never crash into each other – or a flock of birds who also do not crash into each other. There must be some communication or energy at a level we do not consciously comprehend. With the sparrows in the coffee shop, I looked at them in a mood of peace and they sat there and just looked back at me. Who knows what was going on for them but I do think they could pick up on my being at peace with them.

Some Basic Moods

In our work there seem to be six moods that show up predominantly.

Basic Moods of Life

	Peace	Ambition	Wonder
Accept Control	'Accept' Move On	'Could Be' Positive Action	'I Wonder' Exploration
	Resentment	**Resignation**	**Anxiety**
Oppose No Control	'Blame' Revenge	'But' Inaction	'I'm Not Sure' Tentativeness
	Can't Change	*Can Change*	*Uncertainty*

The first two are related to what we perceive we cannot change. One example is history. We cannot change history – what has happened in the past (the phenomena) – but we can help people change their story and their mood about it.

Peace and Acceptance are the moods that show up when we accept that which we assess we cannot change. Today I was in two minds about whether to go for a walk or to continue writing. I decided to go for a walk but then it started to rain heavily; it was cold and I did not have wet weather gear. I could have been annoyed but there was nothing I could do about it; I accepted that I was not going for a walk and continued writing.

Resentment is when we oppose things that we assess we cannot change. People in resentment have a predisposition for revenge, blame and anger. Often when I work with people in this mood their response is, "I will never accept what he/she has done". The issue here is not accepting what they have done, but that it has been done, and nothing can change that.

Ambition in this context means accepting things that we can change and doing something about it – being ambitious!

Resignation is when we oppose things we can change. I have listened to many people say, "What's the point? He's not going to listen to me!" That is resignation. As parents, we must ensure we don't create resignation in our children. We must ensure that we listen to our children's ambitions and not stifle them.

Wonder is where we accept uncertainty. In my assessment, there is more uncertainty in the world today than ever before. In order to survive, we must be creative, innovative, curious, accepting of uncertainty and wonder about where to go and to instil this mood and thinking in our children.

Anxiety is where we oppose uncertainty in life and in relationships. Creativity and innovation will not readily come from anxiety. Anxiety will also limit us to possibilities for change. Anxiety, as an emotion, can serve us well when confronted by a dangerous situation, but once it becomes a long term mood it can become very debilitating.

Resentment, resignation and anxiety all impact significantly in a negative way on productivity. Each alone, or collectively, indicates a perception of no control and consequently will impact seriously on our level of (dy) stress. There is much evidence to suggest that ultimately these three negative moods will have a major detrimental effect on health. I am highly motivated in my work to help all my clients wave goodbye forever to any of these long term negative and self destructive moods.

Moods, Emotions and Our Actions

If we cannot be responsible for our emotion as a result of some event, and we are already in the mood that we observe in ourselves, does this mean we are not responsible for our actions? No, it does not!

I have had many a person say to me they cannot help it – "It is just the way I am!" I claim that when something happens we have an emotional reaction and then there is a moment where we think before we act. I have observed in my clients that sometimes when I challenge them there is a moment where they are clearly emotionally perturbed by me and I think they are going to 'go off' at me, and then they think about it and don't. Most of us sooner or later will be emotionally upset by someone whom we see as a greater authority than ourselves, such as a police officer (or maybe the boss). If we were to allow ourselves to behave from an emotional position such as anger, the perceived consequences have us hold back. There is a fraction of a second where we can think before we act.

In our work with parents who are aggressive, intimidating or 'hot-heads' we have been able to coach them to stop and think between when the emotion shows up and the ensuing reaction. Once we master the awareness of our moods and emotions, and our responses, we can become more mindful of how destructive certain responses can be to relationships and to our own identity. We can then transform and master our intent and choose other, more effective, responses and actions. When mastering this transformation many of our clients have relapses, because we are breaking old habits. Our clients learn that they can learn from relapses. This starts by mastering awareness, and knowing they can go back and have conversations with people involved that will assist in minimizing the damage caused.

Moods as Barriers to Building Relationships

Because of our interpretation of the importance of relationships to effective conversations, I am often called

Moods and Emotions

upon to assist with relationship breakdowns. When people are in conflict, relationships potentially break down and conversations become poor or non-existent. Often the reaction is to get the two into a room and have them talk it out. This can have a degree of success in the short term, which is why it is a common strategy. The next step is to engage a skilled facilitator or mediator and this can also result in some success, especially in the short term. Both are most effective if they occur as soon as possible after the conflict. However, with conflict come a lot of emotions. If the emotions stay around they become a mood, and often one of resentment. If the moods and emotions are ignored – which is often the case – this becomes a barrier to rebuilding relationships. The longer the necessary conversations are ignored, the deeper the mood might become. If we coerce people into having a conversation, this has the potential to feed the resentment. In situations like this, I often start with a conversation with each person individually, and, in the process, listen to the moods, and coach the individual to shift towards a more desirable mood. I then work to help them question how they are observing the situation and how they might be able to observe differently. Only then are they likely to be truly engaged in a conversation about future possibilities with the other person. Often when I work with individuals who are deep in resentment, I observe their desire for revenge. With this comes what I call hand grenades that are being thrown at each other. Until such time as they see the futility of this, they continue to be at war.

With resentment, unfortunately, the only thing that changes is the deterioration of our physical and psychological well-being. I have worked with people who have experienced quite a breakdown when they have come to the realization of the role their mood is playing. My deep-seated concern about resentment is that it can be such a powerful negative mood that it sometimes leads to loss of life. Some become so obsessed with resentment and the desire for revenge that they resort to killing, themselves or others or both.

It was with dismay I recently heard of a twelve year old person who had committed suicide. It became apparent that bullying, harassment and intimidation was involved, both at school and via the various social media. I am sure anxiety and depression was at play here. A key to preventing such tragedies is to have such a relationship with your children that they feel they can come to you in times of such extreme stress. Your relationship must be resilient enough that they feel safe with you and that you will be available to help them. Has your child become more withdrawn or have there been other changes in their behaviour? Your listening is crucial in these situations, including listening to the silence, and listening also to what they want you to do to fix it. Are they petrified that you will rush off to the school and, in their mind at least, make the situation worse?

The key steps for rebuilding relationships are:

- Don't let the issues fester. Encourage conversations as soon as you can and acknowledge emotional content and include it in the conversations.
- If the mood prevails have a qualified person work

with the key players to address moods and to coach them to shift their mood.
- Encourage the conversations to occur, maybe with the assistance of a professional facilitator/coach.
- Engage in a magic wand conversation. If we could wave a magic wand and things could be just how you want them to be, what would it look like? What would be different? What would you and others be saying? Who would be doing what?
- Have each person make effective requests and commitments to each other.

Health and Safety

There is a significant and growing body of evidence to suggest that negative moods have a detrimental impact on our health in the long term. For me this factor alone is ample motivation to be mindful of my moods and emotions and to change them if they are negative.

Moods and emotions also have a significant impact on our safety. I don't think I need to say too much about the relationship between someone being very emotional and their safety. I think most of us know that we should not drive a car if we are very emotional.

In conclusion:

- Moods and emotions play a significant role in how we interact with each other.

- People generally do not, and cannot, readily leave their particular moods and emotions at the front door.

- To bring more appropriate moods and emotions into the home may require some assistance.

- Emotional intelligence is about being mindful of our own moods and emotions, being able to articulate them, and being mindful of the impact they have on others. It is also about how we think about a response to an incident.

- Everyone at some point can decide to stay with an emotional space or not, and to act accordingly or not.

CHAPTER 5: KNOWING OURSELVES; KNOWING OUR CHILDREN

Our children are not us, nor extensions or clones of us. They do not come into the world as a clean slate – they are not like a computer without software. They come into the world with an investigative mind and with a preferred way of processing the information they take in. Unless we observe them this way it is almost impossible to accept how our children differ from each other and from us. They are individuals in their own right from before they are born and it is an imperative that we individualise our parenting style for each child. Yet we continue to raise them according to how we are, how we see the world. So why do we do this and cause so much frustration and anger for ourselves and our children? It starts with not understanding that we only see the world as we are. We do not see the world and our children as they are. We are all different observers and until we really 'get this' we will give both ourselves and our children a stressful time. This is critical to us being happier and, as a result, our children being happier!

Deep down all of us just want to be accepted and understood for whom we are, and this is the greatest gift we can give our children. We are all legitimate, valid human beings and when we embrace the differences in each other and our children our relationships will go to a much deeper and more intimate level. What we are suggesting here is to embrace the quirkiness in each child and stand by them, rather than have them comply and be more like us.

Enhancing your effectiveness, your knowledge, skills and attitudes to parenting can be limited by what you know, and how well you know and take care of yourself. So let us discuss first what we mean by knowing yourself. This is a very interesting area to discuss because, as we discussed in Chapter 2, we are both expanding and conserving. So there is a possibility that you will be a different parent/person after reading this book than you are right now. But you will also be predominantly the same you. So we want to focus on helping you know more about yourself so you can take care of yourself better and, in some instances, expand on who you are, expand on your parenting repertoire. Your memory is your teacher; how you remember being parented is most likely how you will be inclined to parent, whether our parents' way was effective or not. We typically parent with a 'one style suits all' approach, without any regard to the individual child's style. Also, much of what we know and remember is transparent to us; we don't consciously think about it, we just do it. All is done with a very genuine, loving affection and concern for our children and we should not lose sight of that. There is nothing to be gained from being critical of ourselves or our parents for doing what we/they did, which was dependent on what they knew. Yet as with many things, we can always do better.

As we progress through this chapter, we aim to create some breakdowns for you of that transparent way of being, so that you can evaluate and, if you wish, learn to do things in a different way. We will introduce you to some distinctions that you may not currently have, remembering that distinctions give us the opportunity to choose between this and that. We will use two major theoretical bases about human beings, both of which have been validated by substantial research, these being the **Myers Briggs Type Indicator (MBTI) and the Human Synergistics Circumplex**[1].

Myers Briggs Type Indicator (MBTI)

It is not our aim here to go into depth about MBTI as there is so much material readily available via publications and the Internet, and if you are not familiar with it, then we invite you to explore further. One of the many books we do recommend

---

1 Circumplex Styles are copyright ©2011 Human Synergistics International

is *Nurture by Nature: Understand Your Child's Personality Type – and Become a Better Parent* by Paul Tieger & Barbara Barron-Tieger. Just as we now understand that children are born hard wired to be left handed or right handed, it is also critical to understand that we are born with our individual preferences for making sense of our world. Tieger also refers to research that indicates we cannot change our preferences, just as we cannot change our preferences for being right or left handed. In addition, each set of preferences has an order of functions or preferences which not only reflects how we might work through problems but also the order in which we have matured, and our children will mature. This can potentially have a significant impact on our parenting, and on schooling for that matter. Furthermore, instead of parenting according to how we are, we advocate that to ensure the maximum benefits for your children (and yourselves), we must listen to what our children's preferences are and parent according to how they are.

When we coach parents we invite them to complete one of the MBTI preference tests to assist them to understand themselves, their partners and their children. If you don't know your preferences, then we invite you to find a professional who is accredited to use it. The MBTI helps you to identify your preferences for making sense of the world. If not administered correctly and validated by you, it potentially creates confusion between your preferences and your behaviour and, if not explained carefully, it often becomes a label and a self fulfilling prophecy. This can result in you limiting your flexibility and plasticity with your preferences. Let us explain this important point further. MBTI measures your 'preferences' for making sense of the world. A preference means you have options but you might prefer this over that. An MBTI preference is like a gravitational pull to one way, however you can choose to behave differently. You have two hands but you might prefer your right hand over your left. This does not mean you cannot and don't use your left hand. Consequently there is no right or wrong, good or bad.

We have included the following chart, **Your Child's Personality Type**, for you to use, maybe with your partner, to obtain some idea of what your child's preferences are. You then use the corresponding letter to identify the set of preferences. For example, I, Graeme, have preferences towards ENFP, which means E = Extrovert, N = Intuition, F = Feeling, P = Perceptive. Your already listening might be: "Well, are these not labels?" We claim, if used correctly, they are useful distinctions. If someone were to say to me that I have ENFP preferences then I would agree. However, if someone were to say to me I am an ENFP, then I would feel uncomfortable; the inference is that I only behave in a certain way. What is worse, we then often have negative judgements about people and their preferences, which is not helpful.

(E) Extraversion	(I) Introversion
• Energised by being with people • Enjoy big parties • Think out loud, may talk a lot • Don't enjoy playing or working alone • May act first, think later • May appear confident	• Energised by time alone • Enjoy 1:1 interactions • Enjoy the inner world of thoughts • Play happily alone • Think before speaking or acting • May appear inhibited
(S) Sensing (Realist)	(N) Intuition (Dreamer)
• Take in information using the five senses • Understand the world based on past experiences • Can remember facts and details • Enjoy games with rules • Like step-by-step directions or models to follow • Like to play games by the rules	• Take in information using sixth sense • Inspired by possibilities • Notice things that are new or different • Enjoy playing 'make-believe' • Like to use their imagination, hunches, dislike repetition and routine • Like to change the rules as they play
(T) Thinking (Objective)	(F) Feeling (Values-based)
• Use objective thinking and logic to make decisions • Concerned with what is logical and fair • Value consistence, competence • Believe in honesty and may appear blunt • Don't take things personally • May appear unfeeling, selfish, assertive	• Use personal values to make decisions • Concerned with what feels right • Value harmonious relationships • Concerned with other people's feelings and are upset by tension in people • Take everything personally • May lack assertiveness in order to maintain harmony
(J) Judging (Make Plans)	(P) Perceiving (Go with the flow)
• Like to make decisions and have things settled • Like a structured and organised environment • May find changes to plans stressful • Concerned about time – being late, wasting time, how much time is left • Find security in knowing and following rules • Like to finish projects	• Like to gather information and find it difficult to make decisions • Spontaneous and comfortable with the unexpected • Love to explore things that are new • Impulsive, live in the moment, view time as flexible • See rules as barriers to exploration • Like to start projects

Chart 1: Your Child's Personality Type

In brief, the headings refer to:

Extraversion/Introversion:
Where you get your energy from.

Sensing/Intuition:
How you view the world and take in information.

Thinking/Feeling: How you make decisions.

Judging/Perceiving: How you organise your world.

I will now offer you some examples of how this can impact on how we parent.

> In one family the mother has preferences towards ISFP and the father has preferences towards ENFP. Their eldest son has preferences towards ISFJ. When the eldest son was doing homework he would typically work in the quiet of his room, which is also the way his mother would typically work. The father had the tendency to think the way his eldest son was going about homework was not good for him. The second son has preferences towards ENFP so he would do his homework in the presence of others and with either music or TV going at the same time. His mother had the tendency to consider this being the wrong way to do homework. For a more in depth understanding please explore *Nurture by Nature*.

As your children become older and start to consider their careers, listening to who they are and what might work for them is critical. I have coached so many unhappy people who have gone off on a wrong career path and, for many, they see they have little choice about correcting this because of financial and other commitments. Some have been forced by their parents to do what their parents want them to do.

> I coached one young second year university student who came to me primarily to manage his stress levels and associated severe acne. His MBTI preferences were INFP and he was studying law, which he was not enjoying at all. When I inquired as to why he was doing law, he explained that his father was a lawyer and his mother was a doctor of medicine and that he had two choices: medicine or law! What he indicated to me was he really wanted to do fine art, which most likely would have been more aligned to his natural preferences. According to him there was no way his parents would allow him to do that!

In the family example on the previous page, the eldest son spends a large proportion of his career doing research, and the second son is a pastry chef. For a more in-depth understanding perhaps explore, *Do What You Are: Discover the Perfect Career for You Through the Secrets of Personality Type*, by Paul Tieger & Barbara Barron-Tieger.

MBTI preferences have significant implications for children's education and then to their careers as well. As an ENFP, I was very unhappy at school as I was required to read, write, listen, etc., all of which is my less preferred preference of S. In addition, I was required to be logical and analytical which is also my less preferred preference of T. If that was not enough, I was required to have answers, which is also my less preferred P preference. My school was designed by STJ's for STJ's, not an NFP! My schooling was from the 'blank slate treatment' as explained by Lawrence in his book, *Finding the Zone* – follow a tried and true agenda, teach what they need to learn, and then check to make sure they learnt it! No wonder the expansive, investigative mind-set of young children starts to diminish from Year 3 onwards in some educational settings. In the previous family example the eldest son went on to university and earned himself a PhD. The second son hated school and was offered an apprenticeship towards the end of Year 10. He has not looked back since, although there was a strong push by some of his family for him to go onto university like his big brother.

Happier Parents, Happier Children, Happier World

	ISTJ	ISFJ	INFJ	INTJ	ISTP	ISFP	INFP	INTP
DOMINANT	sensing	sensing	intuition	intuition	thinking	feeling	feeling	thinking
AUXILIARY	thinking	feeling	thinking	thinking	sensing	sensing	intuition	intuition
TERTIARY	feeling	thinking	feeling	feeling	intuition	intuition	sensing	sensing
INFERIOR	intuition	intuition	sensing	sensing	feeling	thinking	thinking	feeling
	ESTJ	ESFJ	ENFJ	ENTJ	ESTP	ESFP	ENFP	ENTP
DOMINANT	thinking	feeling	feeling	thinking	sensing	sensing	intuition	intuition
AUXILIARY	sensing	sensing	intuition	intuition	thinking	feeling	feeling	thinking
TERTIARY	intuition	intuition	sensing	sensing	feeling	thinking	thinking	feeling
INFERIOR	feeling	thinking	thinking	feeling	intuition	intuition	sensing	sensing

Chart 2: Order of Preference

Chart 2: The order of preference for each type[2]

While it must be remembered that there is no end point in an individual's development, there are some stages in the development of type. According to Jung, we are born with a predisposition to type, but he also believed the development of traits or preferences is influenced by our upbringing.
In very young children traits can be observed, but the whole point of type development is to consciously use, direct and trust a particular function. Elizabeth Murphy, who is the major theorist and researcher on type and early childhood development, believes children 'test out' the four functions to see which they prefer. At around six to eight (but it could be earlier or later), children settle on a dominant function: this is their most reliable, predictable and useable function. By settling on a dominant function, children also set up their auxiliary function.
    If we have a preference for extraversion, then our dominant function is extraverted and our auxiliary function is introverted.
    If we have a preference for introversion, then our dominant function is introverted and our auxiliary function is extraverted.
    Now let us explore further the preferences and the implications for parenting. To do this we find it helpful to think of each of the eight preferences as having names, e.g. Judging or Perceiving rather than adjectives of how people are. People with a preference for 'Judging' are not necessarily judgemental but prefer the process of making decisions and having things settled. People who prefer 'Perceiving' are not necessarily perceptive but

[2] Geyer, P., *Majors PTI™ Accreditation Course Manual*, 2009

more comfortable and happier in the process of gathering information and going with the flow.

Introverts/Extroverts

If the energy preference of introverts is directed inwards towards concepts and ideas they will more likely want to think and read about it rather than talk about it. Conversely, if the energy preference of extroverts is directed outwards towards people and things, they will more likely want to talk about it. So what are some of the implications for couples and parents? Introverts will think about it, read about it, and will be less inclined to talk to others, or to see all the people around them as a network of help. Under certain circumstances, they may not even notice people when they are out and about. Extroverts want to talk about it and generally notice everybody.

Introvert preference children are often labelled negatively because they may prefer to play alone and not want to join in with others. They may even act aggressively towards siblings or other children when their private space is invaded, especially if they feel they have not had enough time alone. An extroverted preference child may continue to invade the space of the introverted preference child because they want to have more interaction. Typically the introverted child will be the one that is admonished for not playing 'nicely'. Many parents of children with an introvert preference have had early learning centre staff or teachers recommend that their child be tested or assessed, because the child does not fit the norm. There are fewer introverts than extroverts in the world by about 1 in 3.

Introverts must have time alone to recharge their batteries which has significant stress implications for a new parent. Imagine a situation such as with a couple we will call Leanne and Tom.

> Leanne has an Introvert Preference and has a six month old baby, Harriet. Her partner, Tom, has an Extrovert Preference and works full time. Leanne works the equivalent of two and a half days a week and Harriet attends an childcare centre when she works. Before Harriet arrived Leanne managed to get time alone by reading and pursuing her hobbies, although Tom frequently would interrupt her to talk. Her work involves interacting with people. Now that Harriet has arrived she interacts at work, with staff at the childcare centre, with health centre staff and, of course, with Harriet and Tom. She feels like she no longer has any time for herself, that she is on a treadmill and can't get off. Leanne does not naturally think to make requests of others, including Tom or either of their parents or their friends. Her stress levels are building up, although she might not have noticed, except that she is more tearful and feels trapped and depressed. She and Tom have noticed she is getting more impatient with Harriet's demands. Some have suggested she has post natal depression. Tom of course wants to talk to her about it which is the last thing she wants!

Sensing/Intuitive

This dimension concerns the kind of information we naturally notice. People with 'Sensing' preference focus on 'what is' using their five senses, while 'Intuitive' preference people focus on 'what could be'. One of the breakdowns that occur here is about detail versus the big picture. Children with preferences for 'Intuitive' may say to a 'Sensing' preference parent, "What is with all the questions?" We as 'Intuitive' preference people might say to our life partners, "Too much detail!" Of course the reverse also applies. I remember my son (ISFJ) asking me (ENFP) a question, prefaced by, "I want to ask you a question, but I don't want one of your typical psychologist type answers." In other words give me a detailed answer, not another question or big picture philosophical answer.

Often school aged children with an intuitive preference can be labelled as dreamers or labelled as having attention deficit disorder. However, these children may simply be thinking about the future, being creative and feeling impatient with all the detail! I remember when I was five years of age – about the time my intuitive preference would have been close to being fully developed – I had an active imagination and joined bits of string and wire together to trail behind me as a very long passenger train. I also remember claiming to my mother that I knew the driver of a steam train that was coming, and that his name was Tom. Perhaps my mother and father also had an intuitive preference as they would go along with my make-believe stories.

Thinking/Feeling

Previously we suggested embracing the quirkiness in each child and standing by them, rather than having them comply and be more like us. In our experience, both personally and through our work, the Thinking/Feeling preferences are where the greatest invalidation of who we are occurs. This is the only scale where a gender difference exists; research now shows that there is clearly a physiological difference between male and female brains and how the hormones interact with each. We will discuss this later.

On the Thinking/Feeling scale there is much misunderstanding. A person with a 'Feeling' preference uses personal priorities and values as criteria for making decisions. It is reasoning using the relative importance of alternatives, as they affect people and things that are important to us. People with a 'Feeling' preference are better at recognising emotions and taking them into account in decision making. 'Thinking' preference people use impersonal analysis and logic to make decisions and tend to be less in touch with their own and others emotions. Gordon D. Lawrence in his book, *Finding the Zone*, makes these distinctions very clear and understandable.

In western societies at least, males with a 'Feeling' preference have been encouraged by some fathers, uncles, peers, teachers and bosses to act more 'Thinking', to toughen up, and conversely, females with 'Thinking' preferences are encouraged to act more 'Feeling'.

As someone with ENFP preferences, I have a 'Feeling' preference and fortunately for my brother (who also has a preference for 'F') and myself, our father appeared to embrace this difference. I suspect he may also have had an 'F' preference. However, this did little to prepare me for school where my peers and teachers encouraged me to act more 'Thinking'. Many times I felt belittled and that there was something wrong with me and that I was weak. This continued on into the world of work and it was not until I learnt about MBTI did it all fall into place for me. I had very loyal and motivated staff work for me but my boss once told me I was too soft a manager. I started to become much happier about myself once I understood how I am hard wired and that I am a perfectly legitimate, valid, male human being!

In my coaching work, I had a young female engineer do an MBTI preference test and she came out with a very clear preference for 'Thinking'. I asked her if she had ever felt invalidated or not understood in her life. Tears welled up in her eyes and she responded, "Could this be why my mother calls me a heartless bitch, and she has done so ever since I was seven years old?" Her preference for 'Thinking' would have been fully matured at about five years of age!

Judging/Perceiving

'Judging' preference children prefer to live in a fairly structured, organised and planned environment and if one or both parents have a preference for 'Judging' then things will work reasonably well. People with a 'Judging' preference prefer to finish things and it can drive them mad if they, or others, don't finish things, or if anything stops them from finishing. With young children this can show up as disobedience. When it is time to stop doing an activity which is not finished and to move onto something else, the 'Judging' preference child may throw a tantrum or refuse to stop what they are doing. If 'Judging' parents have a child with a preference towards 'Perceiving', then frustrations, tensions and conflict will arise. As you read on, if you have a preference towards 'Judging', then you may well experience some tension just reading about parenting a child with a 'Perceiving' preference. You may also disagree with what we are saying and you may be saying, "No, I disagree, children need to have structure and an organised, planned environment". We could be unsettling you and your 'Judging' preference. You may be demanding your children comply with your expectations.

Children, and adults, with a preference towards 'Perceiving' are often more flexible about everything including time and deadlines. If a child with a 'Perceiving' preference is given a task to complete, conflicts may occur as the child deviates from the task in hand. For example, tidying a room means discovering and playing with toys they might not have played with for a while.

At the weekends, people with a preference towards 'Judging' often have things organised, both for themselves and their children. People with a preference towards 'Perceiving' prefer to have weekends where not too much is organised. Now this is great if all the family has one preference; not so great for those with different preferences.

I recall a teenage boy complaining sadly about how his mum had his life so structured and organised that he had no time to do his own thing. When parenting a 'Perceiving' child you may need to be highly selective about which rules are important and will be enforced and be especially careful about consistency. Otherwise you may get locked into spending too much time and energy reminding, correcting and punishing.

I have coached a number of people who have a very clear preference towards 'Judging', who have not adequately developed their lesser preferred hand towards 'Perceiving'. This has caused them to suffer significant stress, and in some cases depression, considering we live in a world where we can't control everything. In some instances, they have also been parents who are desperately trying to control everything about their children. I encourage them to practise 'sitting on the dock of the bay'.

In summary, remember if you have a preference one way, this does not mean you cannot do the other. If you have a preference towards 'Judging', your preferred hand so to speak, you could use your lesser preferred hand and cut some slack for a person with a preference towards 'Perceiving'. Conversely, a person with a preference towards 'Perceiving' could use their lesser preferred hand and be more structured on occasion. Having said this though, we must remember we are born with our preferences and these will not change; we are hard wired, but we can change our behaviour when we are 'on duty'. When we relax we will revert to our natural preferences, like a gravitational pull. If we force our children to behave in a non-preferenced way and be 'on duty' all of the time, then we will have very unhappy and stressed children and families.

The Human Synergistics Circumplex 9

The Circumplex[3], unlike MBTI, is about learned behaviour and how you have learnt to think about certain situations and your likely subsequent behaviour. The Human Synergistics Life Styles Inventory™ Self-Description (LSI 1) is an instrument that provides feedback on our self-concept – how we think about ourselves and, therefore, the thinking that influences how we approach tasks and interact with others. The Life Styles Inventory Descriptions by Others™ (LSI 2) provides us with feedback from others on how they see us respond under certain circumstances. The completion of the Circumplex comes with a comprehensive Self Development Guide to assist you develop behaviours that are more constructive. In our interpretation parents would become far more effective and happy and have happier children if they strived to be more constructive. The LSI is typically used in corporate settings to assist people understand their leadership styles and behaviour. The reason we use the Human Synergistics models for parenting is that our behaviour most often reflects our childhood origins. In other words, how we were parented has a major influence on how we will parent our children.

3 Circumplex Styles are copyright ©2011 Human Synergistics International

Robin Grille states:

> There are many things that influence the unique ways we care for our children. One of these is information: we all read different books or magazines and we talk to different child health professionals. There are too many cultural practices, social customs and religious beliefs that script our parenting choices, and our temperaments (such as MBTI) imbue the way we respond to our children. But the most powerful influence of all is the way we were parented ourselves.[4]

As with MBTI, it is not the objective of this book to write in depth about the extensive work and research that Human Synergistics has accomplished in this area. Our intention is to expose you to these styles and to create an interruption or breakdown in your transparent way of parenting such that you will consider learning different and more effective styles. This is not to say you or your parents have got it wrong, as we have no doubt that what has gone before in the last few generations has been done in the most caring and affectionate way. Unfortunately we cannot say this about history and if you want to explore how we have evolved as parents, then we invite you to read Robin Grille's books, *Parenting for a Peaceful World* and *Heart to Heart Parenting*. Your parents and their parents did what they did given what they knew. But there is now a possibility that we can become even more effective parents and have a greater influence on creating happier children which may lead to the world being a far more peaceful and happier place. We now have new knowledge and the hindsight of what has gone before us.

4 Grille, R. *Heart to Heart Parenting*, Harper Collins Publishers, 2008, p. 17

I, Graeme, as a qualified psychologist, hypnotherapist and practising meditator, am very aware of a graded range of brain activity in both children and adults. These frequency waves range from the lowest frequency, known as delta waves to higher frequency beta waves. When meditating I am able at times to reach this delta frequency while at other times I go to the next lowest level known as theta frequency. Under hypnotherapy, clients typically can go to the theta level and this helps them to be more open to suggestions and to re-programming. Bruce Lipton in his book, *The Biology of Belief*,[5] cites research where babies between birth and two years of age predominantly operate at the lowest frequency delta waves. Between two and six years of age the child will spend more time in the higher theta frequency. I am explaining this in the hope you will be acutely aware that very young children carefully observe their environment including their parents and significant others, and that this information goes directly into their subconscious memory.

If you can, seek out a qualified administrator of the Human Synergistics Life Styles Inventory (LSI)[6] and have your significant other and yourself complete it. If you cannot find a qualified person, then we invite you to contact Human Synergistics and they will be able to introduce you to someone. You might like to share this information with others, maybe a significant other, and obtain their feedback. If there are other people who have a major role to play in parenting your children, you might invite them to do the same. Please do this in a mood of wonder and curiosity. Listen to each other's responses and see if you recognise where they might fit, but please, we cannot emphasise too

---

5 Lipton, B. *The Biology of Belief*, Hay House, 2008, p. 132
6 Circumplex Styles are copyright ©2011 Human Synergistics International

much, do this in a mood of wonder and curiosity rather than be defensive. This is about moving towards a better way of doing it rather than moving away from what we might have done wrong. The past is complete and we did what we did given the knowledge and skills we had at the time. You might even like to reflect and share how you felt as a child being on the receiving end of this style of parenting, and how you think this has affected the way you are today. Sometimes when we have an adverse reaction to our children, it can stem from a childhood memory of how we felt in similar situations.

Human Synergistics has conducted extensive research and development into the field of individual thinking and behaviour and continues to do so. The Human Synergistics Circumplex presents an integration of a number of different theorists and researchers' work in describing and explaining human behaviour, including Abraham Maslow, Douglas McGregor, Harry Stacks Sullivan, Karen Horney, Carl Rogers and Alfred Adler. The Circumplex in turn is based on the work of Louis Guttman and Timothy Leary and the integration and applied research, determining how to measure these styles and linking them to effectiveness, has been undertaken by J. Clayton Lafferty PhD and Robert A. Cooke PhD. In addition, a special thank you to Shaun McCarthy from Human Synergistics Australia and New Zealand who has used his own knowledge about these styles and the underlying theory and research to build the following information on both 'The Childhood Origins' and 'The Family System'. We thank him for his generosity in allowing us to reproduce much of Shaun's childhood origins work here.

Let's start by carefully working through each of the twelve styles, the first four being the Constructive Styles.[7]

---

[7] Circumplex Styles are copyright ©2011 Human Synergistics International

Constructive Styles

1. Achievement

A family with an achievement style[8] treats children as people, as legitimate valid people given what they know. It is assumed the children have their own way of observing the world, their own wisdom, and can make their own decisions. Children are encouraged to participate in activities that allow them to achieve and their performance is praised not criticised. In sport, it matters not whether you won or lost, but how you played the game. With this focus on doing your personal best and continually improving your skills, there is significantly less likelihood of there being a negative impact on such things as self confidence, self esteem etc. Parents are very supportive and helpful in all that their children are striving to achieve, including supporting them with their dreams. The focus is on outcomes, not weaknesses. By the age of five children are given ample opportunity to try new and different things, they are not closely supervised or protected from failure and they are praised for effort towards doing things well, not punished for doing things poorly. They are taught the importance of the relationship between 'cause and effect' and the impact of certain behaviours on these relationships. They are taught that it is all about the effort they put in; their effort can make a difference no matter what the situation. The outcome for the parents is children who are involved, self reliant, independent

8 Circumplex Styles are copyright ©2011 Human Synergistics International

and successful. For the children, they are self-reliant, self-confident, have high self-esteem and self-worth.

2. **Self-Actualising**

A family with a self-actualised style[9] creates an environment that is creative and does a lot of different and interesting things. Parents talk about what they experienced and how they felt when doing these things, and children are encouraged to do the same. Enjoyable experiences are acknowledged,

9 Circumplex Styles are copyright ©2011 Human Synergistics International

discussed and celebrated. Children are involved in discussions about current events should they wish. Children are included in parental discussions and are treated as unique individuals with their own way of observing the world, their own thoughts and ideas. There is unconditional love where the person is valued for who they are. Love is not performance or activity based and fear is never used as a motivator. Experience is valued and emphasised as an opportunity to learn and grow, mistakes are admitted and corrected without loss of self esteem. Any self put-downs are discouraged as this language can create a negative belief system that becomes part of reality. Any self put-downs are turned into action type conversations. Children are given many opportunities to have their own time, and they are encouraged to figure things out for themselves. Children raised in a self-actualising way are interesting children with a positive self concept, who can easily entertain themselves because they have many interests, and they are confident, self sufficient and independent.

3. **Humanistic-Encouraging**

A family with a humanistic-encouraging style[10] has an emphasis on feelings and close personal relationships, and love is expressed both in words and with physical contact such as hugs; family members are caring and respectful to each other and to all others. They embrace the diversity and differences

10 Circumplex Styles are copyright ©2011 Human Synergistics International

in others (including MBTI differences), so are non judgemental, nor racist, sexist or intolerant. As above, love is unconditional and not performance or activity based. Helping others is the norm, as is talking about how to do it. People are seen as more important than things and conflicts are resolved constructively. Parents show they trust their children and expect that trust to be upheld. Children raised in a humanistic-encouraging style are confident, helpful, independent and loving. They have positive self regard and self esteem and are able to develop non needy relationships.

4. **Affiliative**

A family with an affiliative style[11] is very loving and there is an emphasis on warm family relationships. People are valued as more important than things and others are talked about in a friendly, warm and respectful manner. Friendships are highly valued so the family has many friends to visit and children are encouraged to mix with as many different types of people as they can. There is always an 'open house' for friends from an early age through to teenage years and beyond, where friends are valued and not criticised. Once again, love is unconditional and not performance or activity based. As a consequence, children have a lot of strong friendships and are well socialised. In addition, the children's friends react positively to parents.

---

11 Circumplex Styles are copyright ©2011 Human Synergistics International

Passive/Defensive Styles

5. Approval

We are now moving into the domain of the Passive/Defensive Styles. A family that has an approval style[12] is overly concerned with outward appearances and impressing others, and has a focus on what others think (e.g. friends, neighbours, colleagues at work etc.). What you look like is emphasised and pleasing and impressing others is expected. If we don't feel we can impress others, or if someone does something to 'disgrace' the family, then this is terrible. A family that has an approval style may also have dominant parents who use love or absence of love as reward or punishment, and parents who demand their children respect them. 'Correct' behaviour is rewarded and 'incorrect' behaviour is punished and the reasons for reward and punishment are seldom explained to the child. Children learn to not disagree, or upset, those who have the power to reward or punish them. A further scenario could be where one parent is dominant and the other encourages the children to not upset dad/mum. This can sometimes be played out by one parent being the disciplinarian, "Just wait until your father gets home!" Most often in this environment there is little or no approval. Consequently, the children appear loving and obedient as they will say and do anything to gain approval; they rarely engage in any conflict or disagreement. The children are insecure in relationships and any relationship breakdowns are 'my fault'. Children feel their self regard is conditional on whether they have the approval of others.

12 Circumplex Styles are copyright ©2011 Human Synergistics International

6. **Conventional**

A family that has a conventional style has an environment that is structured and orderly and individuals are expected to conform to social expectations and values set by others. Children are forced to apologise when they don't really mean it. There are many rules about what and how things should be done. There is an excessive emphasis on promptness: running lives by the clock. 'Appearing normal' and 'well rounded' is emphasised and others are judged against this standard. There is rigid discipline, an emphasis on being clean and tidy, and conflict is strongly discouraged. Some typical messages by parents are, "You ought to be ashamed of yourself" or "Because the bible tells us so" or "Because the teacher said so". Parents believe others will judge them well because of how good their children are, as they will have well behaved, obedient, clean, neat and tidy children. However, there are costs for the children; they will lack creativity or original thinking, they will be conforming – but can excel in a conforming environment, and they will be insecure in relationships.

7. **Dependent**

A family that has a dependent style[13] has an autocratic environment with an emphasis on punishment without explanation, and very little reward. It has an emphasis on 'moving away from', "Stop doing that" as opposed to 'moving towards', "In future, could you please ..." In Chapter 12 we discuss this in greater

13 Circumplex Styles are copyright ©2011 Human Synergistics International

depth with regard to making effective requests. Children are not allowed to make decisions and are under 'strict instructions' on almost everything. There is little or no explanation of events and situations, and children are 'made to be seen but not heard'. Parents design and manage the children's environment without any involvement from the children as they believe they always know what is best for their children, even to the extent of what they should/shouldn't be interested in ("they are too young to understand"). This is an environment that has a dominant parent(s) and/or older sibling; children are over protected (without any conversations with children). There are minimal opportunities for risk, little opportunity for decision making and minimal opportunities for learning life skills. There is a high focus on an external locus of control, e.g. "There is nothing we can do about it", and frequent references to luck, chance, magic, fate or bad karma. Parents will use excuses and blame others and will often play practical jokes on children. This style will produce obedient, undemanding children who will comply with parents who have all the power. However, the children will feel powerless and helpless; they will be insecure, lack confidence, and lack cause and effect thinking.

8. Avoidance

A family that has an avoidance style[14] is characterised by dominant (anxious?) parenting where fear of failure is emphasised rather than the possibility and opportunity to succeed. Everything is done for

---

14 Circumplex Styles are copyright ©2011 Human Synergistics International

the child as they are seen as too young, not strong enough, not clever enough or good enough to do it, so they have no opportunity to attempt difficult tasks. Children are ignored and expected to keep out of the way, usually deal with very harsh criticism from dictatorial parents, where failure is dwelt on and seen as a measure of self worth. Shortcomings are criticised and/or punished and there are no rewards or recognition for any achievements. Anxiety is the norm and is even encouraged as good for you. There are many fear of danger messages – the world is a dangerous place, complaining about life in front of the children, and plenty of overt worry by parents about everything a child does. The consequences are obedient children where parents feel in control and believe it is easier to do it themselves. The children will feel insecure, will lack confidence, fear authority, and avoid any risk taking and thus much of life's experiences.

Aggressive/Defensive Styles

9. Oppositional

We are now moving into the domain of the Aggressive/Defensive Styles. A family that has an oppositional style[15] is focused on the negative; it is predominately cynical and sceptical and criticism of others is reinforced. A parent uses a taunting style with children believing it is funny and children are

---

15 Circumplex Styles are copyright ©2011 Human Synergistics International

encouraged to comment on each other's faults as a source of family humour. Children are frequently compared or tested against others, but are not recognised or given any satisfaction from the results achieved. There is much laughing at children and minimal praise. Cynicism is a way of being seen and noticed in a family. There are usually dominant parent(s) and one parent may be critical of another in front of children. The result for children is they find it difficult to form close relationships, they are constantly looking at what's wrong. As a consequence they have low self worth, anger is their predominant mood and they see little pleasure in the world.

10. **Power**

A family that is power oriented[16] has an environment that is very controlling and rigidly disciplined by dominating parent(s) where respect for parents, elders or those in authority is emphasised. Parents use scare tactics to teach that respect. If only one parent is dominant, children identify with the parent who dominates the other. Parent(s) exercise power without explanation and decisions are made for the children. The family environment is very judgemental where class, race, locality etc. are talked about and judgements passed accordingly. Strong prejudices are the norm. Generally it is a very argumentative environment where differing judgements or truths

16 Circumplex Styles are copyright ©2011 Human Synergistics International

meet head on and children learn to be tough to survive. Parents can become very defensive and upset when children raise an opposing view and generally refuse to listen to their opinions. The result is children appear obedient, respectful and tough. The cost for the children is they lack self confidence which is reflected in their posture which can be off centre, with round shoulders and head down. They are insecure in relationships and their ego is attached to tasks.

11. **Competitive**

A competitive[17] family environment is very much focused on winning and never losing. Parents talk about winners and losers and children are pushed into sports and then compared with others with the focus on being the best. Competition is the way of gaining parents' approval and recognition. The emphasis is on winning and losing rather than on the experience. Parents may well compete to win children's approval. Competitive thinking is all about asserting your superiority over others. With winning and losing, a lot is at stake when you lose, such as loss of confidence, low self-worth, low self- esteem, frustration, plus negative moods such as resentment towards other competitors, resignation, "I am never going to be any good at this!" and performance anxiety. Competitive thinking people have to protect

[17] Circumplex Styles are copyright ©2011 Human Synergistics International

themselves from these very things. This protection causes them to have a tendency towards aggression, becoming defensive about feedback as criticism is seen as an attack on their esteem. In addition, competitive oriented people always have to perform in almost everything they do; they often lack self motivation and friendships are superficial.

12. **Perfectionistic**

A family that has a perfectionistic thinking style[18] has an environment that is demanding, has rigid discipline and very high expectations for performance that are unrealistic, especially for children. Children (who become adults!) learn that nothing is ever good enough. Children are expected to be the best at everything and mistakes or failures are not acceptable. The perfectionistic family will have an unemotional environment where emotions are avoided and ignored and where love is not expressed. People are assessed on the basis of what they do and how much they earn. Worth is linked to how successful people are. The result is that children appear to be hard working high achievers, but they are unable to deal with emotions and are never satisfied with their achievements and accomplishments

To reiterate, there is no more powerful influence on how we parent than that of how we were parented. In addition, if

18 Circumplex Styles are copyright ©2011 Human Synergistics International

our grandparents are actively involved in raising children, then these styles will continue unless we actively change our styles and the styles of those who are involved in raising our children.

In conclusion:

- What we offer you is based on the knowledge that we are all different observers of the world.

- We can use MBTI as a framework for understanding the differences between people.

- We believe the most effective way of parenting lies in the 'Constructive' style, and most of the content of this book is how to do that.

- We acknowledge that we are all legitimate, valid human beings.

- We recognise a vital component of good parenting is for parents to take care of themselves.

CHAPTER 6: CARING FOR OURSELVES; CARING FOR OUR CHILDREN

In order to enhance how effectively we take care of ourselves and our children we need to be mindful of what we currently do to manage both our wellbeing and our children's wellbeing. The key to taking care of ourselves is all wrapped up in what we call managing stress. If we don't take care of ourselves and/or our children then we will have stress. We find that a high level of stress, in both parents and children, has a major detrimental effect on health and all aspects of families and parenting. At one level we all know about stress and what it is to be 'stressed out'. We will discuss this important topic and its relevance to all aspects of parenting.

What is Stress?

If we refer you to Figure 1, **Stress & Performance**, an interpretation originally offered by Yerkes & Dodson, you will notice that stress can be broken up into two subsets; there is good stress (Eustress) and there is bad stress (Dystress). Our aim when we talk about managing your stress is to have you be in the good stress as much as is possible, given the circumstances you find yourself in. When you go into bad stress we want you to initially be mindful that this is where you are, and to understand what you can do to get more balanced and back into good stress as soon as possible. In our interpretation, an expectant mother who manages her stress will be in a far better position when she goes into labour to cope with the stress of it all than an already stressed mother. In addition, because the baby is attached to the mother via the placenta, the baby will also be better able to cope with the stress of being born.

When we are under dystress for a period of time we can become depressed, so it is possible that post natal depression could be averted or minimised if the mother actively manages her levels of stress. A baby and a mother who are both dystressed are not a good combination. The baby will become even more dystressed as he picks up on the mother's dystress. The reasons and motivation to change will become even more apparent to you as we go on.

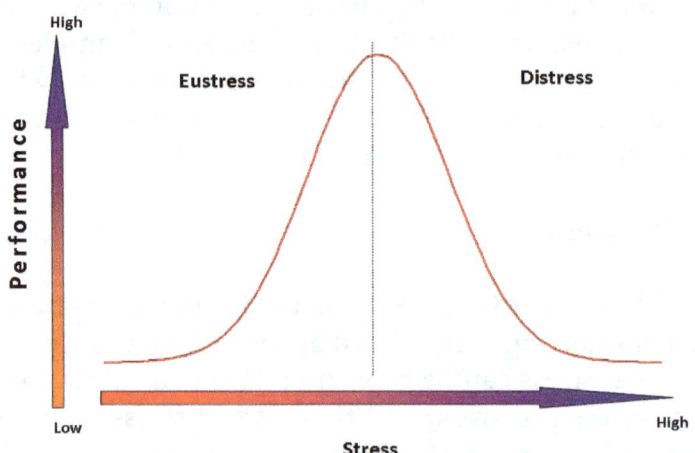

Figure 1: Stress and performance

If we have good and bad stress then obviously we must need some stress almost all the time. As I, Graeme, sit here at the computer writing this, I have the stress (motivation) that drives me to write and I have enough stress to be sitting upright; all good stress. I claim it is good stress that had me go for a bike ride this morning and have a light lunch. I have done much to reduce the negative stress. I have not quite worked out what to do about the house telephone ringing! So I would claim I am cruising along, which is a good place to be. This gives me some reserves for when that extra effort is required.

What do I mean by that? For example, if I am driving my car I am probably using some more good stress but still cruising which is very handy when I have to take some evasive action. My body will react with a shot of adrenaline and I will cope with the situation. If I am over in the dystress side I may not be as effective with my action and may panic. In addition, I will be far more inclined to be angry at the other driver and I may engage in road rage. We are all different observers and we all make mistakes! People predisposed to road rage are not managing their stress levels effectively.

Stress is the body's mechanism for our survival and the survival of our offspring and it worked very effectively when we were a species in the wild. We either fought hard or ran hard, both of which used up our adrenaline. When we sensed the danger had passed we did what all the other animals do – relax and do nothing. With all animals, including ourselves, when we are totally physically and mentally relaxed, the brain sends out signals and our body releases chemicals; these chemicals neutralize our adrenaline and it is released through our urine. In modern society many do very little to burn this up or relax. For the remainder of this chapter, when we refer to stress and being stressed we are referring to the dystress or bad stress side.

Where does stress live?

In our interpretation, stress lives in **three broad domains.**

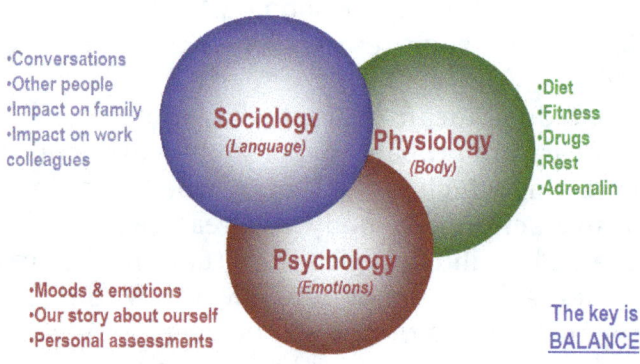

One domain is what we call the *sociology* or *our society*. As human beings we exist in language and it is our conversations and relationships with others that cause stress, in varying degrees. Having a conversation typically involves other people. Some of these conversations have us feel good about ourselves and others can have us feel stressed. If we have a parent-teacher meeting and we are told that our son or daughter is doing well at school, then we feel great. Even if we are asked to spend a little more time with our child over a certain aspect of their schooling we will most likely be motivated. But what if the teacher says you need to have your child tested for whatever? Then we may not feel so great. What is the impact on our stress levels if we are criticized about our parenting, directly or indirectly? The quality of our conversations and behaviour is dependent on our levels of stress. If we arrive home after a stressful day, then as soon as we walk in the door almost everything starts to irritate us.

The second domain is our *physiology* – our body. Our diet, fitness level, drugs, amount of rest and adrenaline all puts stress on our body in both the short term and the long term. Today, because I am predominantly sitting and writing I had a light lunch and went for a bike ride. I have rest breaks when I do various relaxation exercises and I don't take non prescribed or illicit drugs. In addition, as coffee is a stimulant to the adrenal glands I limit myself to two cups maximum per day and rarely after three p.m., as I find this can impact on the quality of my sleep.

The third domain we call our *psychology*, or *our story* about ourselves, including our personal assessments and how we feel about ourselves. Do I believe I am an okay person, and in all areas of my life? Am I a good father, or a good coach, or a good husband, etc.? Am I a worthwhile person? Throughout this book we discuss elements of parenting that enhance our children's sense of worth and self esteem.

These three domains all overlap because there is always interplay between them, and all have an impact on our moods and emotions. Managing stress is about working towards balance between all domains. If I keep to a balanced diet, maintain a level of fitness, ensure I get adequate and effective rest and ensure a good balance of adrenaline, then I am far less likely to want prescribed or non prescribed drugs. If I believe I am an okay person, then I am more likely to cope with my interactions and conversations with others.

Some of the symptoms of stress (Dystress):

Physiological

When we are under stress for a period of time without managing it (see below for some techniques for managing stress), our immune system starts to become less effective. For those of you who may have had your mother say to you when you have a cold, "You must be run down", intuitively she was right. Our bodies provide us with plenty of clues about our levels of stress, if we would just be mindful of them.

Some of the more common early signs of stress are just the feeling of irritability and/or zero tolerance to other people and/or things. This might be accompanied with a headache or pain in the neck and/or shoulders. You may have tension in your jaw or be grinding your teeth. It may show up as a redness of your skin on your face or neck.

If left unattended then more severe symptoms will start to show, depending on your predisposition. I, Graeme, have the predisposition to have psoriasis of the skin which is normally under control because I actively manage my levels of stress. I also have had a history of colds, influenza and sinusitis, which I have minimized. I have an allergy to dust, grass clippings, and some paints and glues. The result used to be nasal congestion and often severe sinusitis. I still have the allergies but the reaction is close to zero.

The long term consequences of high levels of stress can contribute to more serious illnesses such as high blood pressure, heart attacks, strokes and cancers etc. (Keeping in mind the three domains, and not forgetting that under *physiological* is our diet and fitness levels).

Psychological

Our psychological wellbeing is directly related to our levels of stress. When under stress we are agitated, irritable and quick to become angry or anxious and depressed. Our assessments of ourselves and others tend to be focused on the negative, and as a consequence, our concept of ourselves and our self esteem can rapidly decline. In addition, it all feels as though it is just too hard. We become de-motivated to do almost anything, and we want to withdraw from the world. For many, sleep becomes a way of withdrawing from the world. Unfortunately, some even contemplate suicide. As stated previously, this is not a good place for a parent to be, not only for themselves but for their children. You become unapproachable to your children, and you are unlikely to be listening to them. Your stress most likely is creating stress in them and they may well be displaying some of the symptoms outlined above.

Emotional

When we are stressed we become very emotional. In Chapter 4 we discussed in greater depth managing moods and emotions. In our interpretation emotions happen as a result of something; they are reactive to an event. If the emotion stays with us then it becomes a mood and we are always in a mood. If you stop right now and reflect, what mood are you in right now and is it serving you well? Throughout this book we want to encourage you to be mindful of what is happening to you right now, both internally and externally, and what might be happening between you and your children, because moods are very contagious! Under stress we are drawn to what we typically say are negative moods, for example, resentment, resignation, anxiety etc. So when we are stressed and we become very emotional, little things set us off. Be mindful of these signs and take some action to manage your stress, which we outline below.

Behavioural

When we are stressed our behaviour can polarize and we are not our normal selves, although if you have not been managing your stress for a long time, you and others may not know your 'normal self'! In Chapter 5 we introduced you to the Human Synergistics Thinking Styles, and the Aggressive Defensive styles are closely linked to the fight of stress. This was fine when we needed to fight to save ourselves, protect our young, and/or get something to eat. Now we lead very sedentary lives compared to lives in the wild so it comes out in other ways. Similarly, the Passive Defensive styles are closely linked to the flight of stress, where we ran as fast as we could to save ourselves. Once again, we lead very sedentary lives compared to lives in the wild so it comes out in other ways. We might feel like running away from it all but most of the time we can't!

In terms of behaviour, this translates into aggressive behaviour or withdrawing. Aggressive behaviour can be quick to anger and/or violence, physical or psychological intimidation and bullying, road rage, smashing things etc. Withdrawing behaviour is sulking, retiring to the bedroom or going to bed too often, depression, or literally running away and hiding. People may go from one to another.

Caring for Ourselves; Caring for our Children

Aggression

We also engage in other sorts of behaviour, such as drinking (more?) alcohol and drinks containing caffeine. Remember that caffeine stimulates the adrenal glands, which means more adrenaline, not less. We may take a drug for a headache or other prescribed or non prescribed, legal or illegal drugs, all of which add to the body's stress. Before I learnt how to meditate I used to head for the bar when I had a headache, which was always a precursor for sinusitis. The headache went after a couple of alcoholic drinks but I didn't feel great the next morning! Then I learnt to meditate when I had a headache and it would go away; now I don't get them. Others may eat less or eat more or go on binges.

Happier Parents, Happier Children, Happier World

Person withdrawn

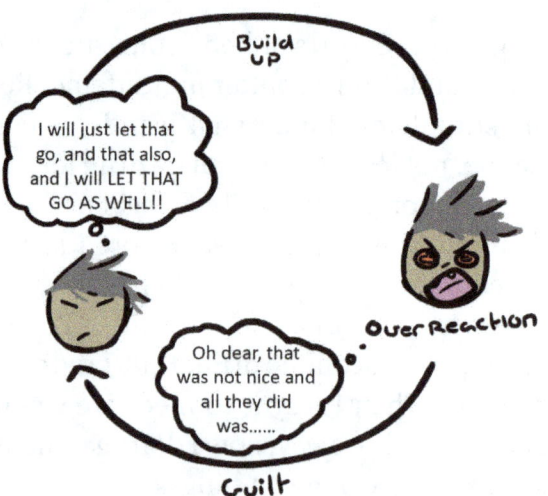

Keep it up and eventually spin out of control.

Passivity Cycle

Strategies for Managing Stress

Diet

Some of you may be very conscientious about your diet so you may well want to skip over this part. For the remainder, this book is not about healthy diets and our purpose here is to simply raise your awareness of diet and its impact on stress. High levels of caffeine, as mentioned above, all raise your levels of stress. Alcohol (or anything to excess), all puts more stress on your body. It is well documented that some wine is actually good for you, which is certainly an interpretation that we like to subscribe to! Having said this, though, I do subscribe to having some days that are alcohol free, to not only give your liver and body a break, but also to ensure you have some nights where your REM (Rapid Eye Movement) sleep is not impaired. A lot of packaged and take-away food has questionable healthy food standards. Low Glycaemic Index (Low G.I.) foods and a good balanced diet are ideal for all kinds of reasons, not only for stress management but also for long term good health. For women that are pregnant it is useful to remember your baby is very much part of you as it is connected via the placenta, so what you eat or drink will also be impacting on your baby. Your moods and emotions also affect your baby.

Exercise

If you are fit then you can skip over this section. However, we are speaking to those of you who lead quite sedentary lives for all sorts of reasons. In our work in the corporate world we see so many people who work from dawn until dusk and do no exercise. There are all kinds of problems with this, none the least being the lack of exposure to some sunlight which can contribute to depression (or winter blahs as is often quoted)! Many psychologists in private practice find they have a peak in early spring of clients suffering from depression. At work the more pressure or stress, the harder people try to work, and the less effective they become so the longer they work to try to compensate! What we are strongly advocating is thirty minutes on average of exercise each day. A brisk walk is all that it takes. Maybe go swimming. Anything more is even better! Go for a walk at lunch time or park the car and walk. When you have babies, take them with you in a pram or sling, toddlers in a stroller, and once they can walk a combination of having them run, walk and then retreat to the stroller. They will also get into the habit of getting exercise. The added benefit for children is being exposed to new experiences – the birds, trees, wind, sun, clouds, animals, the stars and the moon. The world offers a rich environment. Apart from all the other benefits of exercise it also burns up the unspent adrenaline.

Meditation

When we say meditation, we are referring to any activity that has the mind and body totally relaxed, and we don't include watching TV or reading, as the mind is still active. There is a whole range of material available as well as different techniques. I first experienced meditation when I was on a workshop and the facilitator took us through a relaxation exercise. I found it wonderful! I then became exposed to more techniques in my undergraduate clinical psychology. Following this I learnt some of my techniques from audio recordings. If you are using CD's etc. that are using speech to take you through, try after a few times of listening to simply relax with the sound of the voice.

When I am in a totally relaxed state, both physically and mentally, I also use what is known as *guided imagery* and I use this for all sorts of things, such as rehearsing in my mind some event in the future going well. Currently I have slight early symptoms of a cold, a tickle in the throat. Today in my relaxation exercise I imagined breathing in the air over my throat and that it is cleansing it. When I breathe out I imagine a cloud of infected germs being blown away. From my past experiences, I don't believe this cold will advance to any significant degree.

There are many different forms of meditation available, some are sitting, some lying down. I prefer lying down as I find I can relax all my muscles and can imagine sinking into the floor, and when I get to the near deepest level, it is as if a wave has washed over me and I go even deeper. In my work with others I find that some of my clients have mini-naps and do not seem to have the distinction to identify the difference between being in a very relaxed state and a light sleep. Others say that when using relaxation CD's they fell asleep. However, when I ask a few questions they come to realize they were not asleep, simply in a very relaxed state.

When you are taking care of yourself and your stress levels, you will become a more relaxed person and consequently people around you will become more relaxed, including babies and children. In addition, when you learn the distinction between relaxed and stressed, you can assist your children by talking to them in a calm relaxed voice, or by playing some relaxation music.

Massage

A relaxation massage by a professional masseuse is wonderful for inducing a totally relaxed state, whether it is just neck and shoulders or a full body massage. I have a full massage once a month and in addition to inducing a totally relaxed state, it also sorts out where in my body I am holding some stress; sometimes in my neck and/or shoulders, sometimes in my jaw, sometimes in the muscles in the lower back. If you have experienced how wonderful this sensation is you can also gently introduce it to babies and children. Once you know how great it feels to have your neck, or back, or forehead, or top of the head, or hands massaged, (the list goes on) you can gently massage your baby or child and watch the results!

Time out

Sometimes in our lives we just simply need to take time out from whatever it is we are doing, and parenting is no exception. How do you do that when parenting is a 24/7 thing, I hear you ask! Well, for a start the whole world is a network of help, just waiting to be tapped into, starting with grandparents, aunties, uncles, friends and neighbours, just to mention a few. Then what do you do with time out? Well we have already mentioned exercise, meditation, massage, or doing what you love, or simply having time alone to recharge your batteries.

Agreed boundaries, rules and limitations

As parents, it is very useful for managing the stress of the family to have agreed boundaries, rules and limitations. The emphasis here is on agreed, at least between the parents, and the children, depending on their age. If there is no agreement then stress comes into play over who is right! These boundaries, rules and limitations don't need to be too narrow or too tight, as you don't want to stifle the investigative nature of children, but at the same time you do want to ensure their safety and wellbeing. If we are too paranoid we will not let children out of our sight, or if we are too reckless, they can go and play on the railway line! If we have very tight boundaries, rules and limitations, then we have children who have been overprotected; they may not know what to do in certain situations. A common one is to instil in children not to talk to strangers. Children are better prepared for situations if we play out 'what if' scenarios with them. As Gordon Lawrence discusses in his book, *Finding the Zone*, parents and children can partner up in an investigation as to how to find a trustworthy adult who can help in certain situations. This way, we teach the child to be cautious about situations rather than people.

Once we have agreed boundaries, rules and limitations, it becomes easier to focus on the major deviations and not stress out over the small ones. For example, a new born baby knows how to close her hand and hold things. As a baby develops, she discovers letting go of things, and the investigative nature of the baby enjoys the experience and wants to practise it! However, when this involves dropping food or a cup on the ground we admonish her! If we observe it as investigating and practising, rather than the baby being naughty, then we might partner the baby in the investigation. If it involves making a mess then put a plastic sheet down to protect the carpet. Does it matter if we have a bit of mess to clean up off the tiled floor?

Our stories and assessments about ourselves, about our babies and children, and about our significant others

We engage in conversations for stories and assessments most of the time, and for most of this time we think we are describing how things are. What we are not generally aware of are the traps involved, and these traps apply as much to parenting as to any other aspect of our lives. We will discuss this in far greater depth in Chapter 10 which we have devoted to this topic.

One thing we do offer here is to be observant and mindful about a mother's stories and assessments about feeding her baby, about breast feeding or about broken sleep. We all know that a baby requires feeding after short periods of time and the mother's story about this will have a significant impact on both the mother and baby's stress levels. It is natural for a baby to require regular feeds throughout the night. How the mother approaches this can have a positive or negative effect on both with regard to stress. You know you will have interrupted sleep so plan for it accordingly. What is your story when the baby wakes you in the middle of the night? What is your assessment during the day? "Oh, I am so tired!" When we make these assessments we think we are describing how we feel. However, in doing so we are also creating that we feel tired. What we want to point out here is the impact these conversations can have on our levels of stress.

In this chapter we have aimed to show you that an imperative to being happier parents who have happier children is to prioritize taking care of yourselves, and, of course, your children.

In conclusion:

- Our levels of stress affect not only ourselves, but also those around us.

- The quality of our conversations and behaviour are dependent on our levels of stress.

- Under stress we are drawn to negative moods and over time, stress can lead to depression.

- Time management involves setting priorities and maybe the ability to ignore tasks that can wait.

There are a number of areas in our lives where we can change our behaviour to mange stress more effectively. These are:

- Exercise
- Meditation
- Massage
- Time out
- Our own rules and limitations
- Our stories and assessments of ourselves, babies/children, significant others
- Different conversations

CHAPTER 7: RAISING GIRLS

We have decided to separate this next topic into two parts, raising girls and raising boys. Some of you may be thinking that this is wrong and we should not do this. Again we ask that you remain open to what has been written and be in a mood of curiosity and wonder.

There are many reasons for this decision and as you read through this chapter and the next we hope that you become aware of many of these, and their relevance to bringing up children.

One of the reasons came to light over sixty years ago when a mother and daughter were initially developing a theory and a set of questions about human nature. This was the nucleus of the thinking and theory we now know as the Myers Briggs Type Indicator (MBTI) which we have discussed previously. When developing their theory and testing it they discovered that all women had a 'Feeling' preference and all males had a 'Thinking' preference. But they were convinced that there was something else going on here and they hypothesised that this was because females are traditionally in the nurturing role. So what Myers Briggs did was to weight it such that it has now a 60/40 distribution. Sixty per cent of females score a preference of 'Feeling' and forty per cent of males score a 'Feeling' preference. What we didn't know then but do know now is that there is a physiological difference between male and female brain structure. Because of this weighting and the physiological difference we could assume that a male with a very clear preference for 'Thinking' will be far more that way than a female counterpart. Conversely, a female with a very clear preference for 'Feeling' will be more so than a male counterpart. However, this Thinking/Feeling distinction is insufficient to explain all the gender differences, as Alison will explain.

Raising Girls

When Graeme invited me to write about raising girls, I asked the question, "Why are we writing a separate section about raising girls, and one on raising boys?" After all, we believe all children have special needs and should be raised according to their needs.

It took me some time to clarify the issue in my mind. As a student of Women's Studies in the early 90's when the nature/nurture debate was an issue, I firmly sided with the nurture side, believing that the differences in how we raise girls and boys was the deciding factor in how children developed gender differences. I have since changed my viewpoint and believe both play a part. My own parenting experience, together with evidence from recent advances in technology, has provided me with more information.

As we all know, men and women are designed differently. Traditionally, men and women had very different roles due to this design. Men were hunters and protectors; women were gatherers and nurturers. What I find interesting is the biological differences that may have brought about these roles. Men needed to be bigger and stronger, with the spatial skills that allowed them to navigate and hit a moving target. Groups of women used their peripheral vision to monitor for danger and used landmarks to navigate in the landscape close to home. Their ability to sense changes in the behaviour and appearance of others allowed them to co-operate with each other and identify illness.

Tools such as PET and MRI scans now allow us to document "... an astonishing array of structural, chemical, genetic, hormonal and functional brain differences between men and women."[1]

These differences, combined with the way we treat girls, the language we use when talking to them, the toys we provide and many other variations on nurturing styles, create real differences in the way we raise girls and boys.

Most of the brain development that determines gender-specific differences occurs in the first half of pregnancy. A girl's brain has a larger communication centre and also more connections in the areas that process emotions. What does this mean for the newborn baby? There is a lovely exercise, sometimes referred to as eye gazing, where you make eye contact with a newborn baby and mirror her expressions and the sounds she makes. This exercise is considered to be an important way to strengthen the bond between babies and their carers. Recent research has found that eye gazing is an activity suited to baby girls but not one that especially interests baby boys. Girls are wired to study faces and make eye contact.

[1] Brizendine, L., *The Female Brain*, Transworld Publishers, 2007, P. 4

Baby girls are also more interested in emotional expression. They are more skilled than baby boys at interpreting emotions, particularly from facial expression. A baby girl will develop with a sense of self that is largely based on her interpretation of emotional expression she receives from people she is close to. "But take away the signposts that an expressive face provides and you've taken away the female brain's main touchstone for reality."[2]

A baby girl, to generalise, is more responsive to non-verbal cues than a baby boy. To receive the emotional support she needs, a baby girl will look at the faces of her carers for feedback. She needs your calming presence when she is upset and your smiles when she is happy.

Once again we return to the topic of support for mothers of newborn babies. In my experience it is an impossible task to single-handedly provide the level of physical and emotional care that a baby girl needs, and has the right to need! I do not believe it is possible to 'spoil' a baby; she is defenceless and completely dependent on her

---

2 Brizendine, L., *The Female Brain*, Transworld Publishers, 2007, P. 4

carers. You can best nurture your baby girl when it feels pleasurable. When you feel exhausted and isolated, the quality of your care diminishes. This in turn may cause you to feel angry, resentful and guilty, which your baby girl will pick up on. She is likely to react to this by becoming upset, which causes you more stress, and so the cycle goes. That's why parents need to feel supported and to have their own emotional needs met.

The reality of our culture for many families living in Australia is that of the nuclear family. I personally wish it wasn't the case. Despite attending ante-natal classes and reading books, many first-time mothers have no idea what to expect when they bring their baby home from hospital. Even with support from family and friends, the experience of being a mother for the first time can be exhausting, isolating and stressful.

A woman I spoke with recently, Lisa, described her experience. At the time she was living in a small country town, away from her immediate family. Her baby's crying and her inability to comfort her caused her enormous stress. This reaction probably came from a number of causes; certainly lack of knowledge, confidence and support were contributing factors. According to Robin Grille in his book *Heart to Heart Parenting*, the way our mothers felt with a newborn baby impacts on our responses and this may well be the case. Fortunately for Lisa and her baby, a neighbour stepped in and took the baby between several feeds every day for the first few weeks and Lisa had a much-needed break at these times. There was also a wonderful infant welfare sister who introduced Lisa to baby massage and started up a playgroup, which Lisa described as a welcome support in an isolated community.

As your baby becomes a toddler, she continues to

need a secure attachment and also your understanding of her developing need for independence. At this time – from around twelve months to four years – she is attempting many new tasks. I know I experience high levels of frustration from time to time when I am learning new skills, and it is no different for your daughter. With this increased independence comes increased anger and frustration! So what is a tantrum? I see it as an expression of extreme frustration. An opposing belief is to focus on the behaviour, which may be described as unreasonable/attention seeking/manipulative.

A client, whom I will call Sue, was talking about her daughter's tantrums. Her belief was that her daughter's tantrums were attention seeking behaviour and she believed the best way to manage this was to ignore the behaviour. Even if this is the case, how do you feel if you are extremely angry/frustrated/upset and the person you are 'venting' to walks out of the room? Does this increase and/or redirect the feelings you are experiencing? What do you need at the time? For me, I want to be heard. One of the ways we calm ourselves is to talk (or shout!) through an issue with someone we are close to. They don't usually need to solve the problem, but they do need to listen. If you view a tantrum as out-of-control feelings, your response may be different. Sue found that, over time, her ability to respond with empathy to her daughter's tantrums reduced the frequency of the behaviour.

The female brain is built for connection. Because we respond naturally to the strengths in our children, our responses to a girl's needs means we constantly reinforce and strengthen the neural pathways for connection with others. As a girl grows, her ability to use and understand language develops faster than that of boys. According to

Gisela Preuschoff in her book, *Raising Girls*, girls aged ten to sixteen months have a vocabulary that is approximately double that of boys of the same age. As parents we respond to this strength, thereby nurturing language development in girls.

Because girls' language and social skills develop earlier than boys', there is also an observable difference in the way that young children play. A girl is 'wired' to form close relationships. Watch pre-school aged children playing and you will see a marked difference in behaviour. Girls tend to enjoy games that involve a level of nurturing and they are also much better at sharing and taking turns than boys. I had a conversation recently with a client who has a three year old daughter who attends kinder. She disagreed with what she considers to be a stereotypical view of gender differences, and told me that her daughter's favourite toys are building blocks. When we talked in more detail about this activity, she told me that her daughter and several other girls used the blocks to build houses for dolls, or zoos and farms for family groups of plastic animals. The boys almost invariably turned any construction toy into a weapon or vehicle.

Girls are not, however, 'sugar and spice and all things nice'; some girls are 'bossy' and want everything their own way. While a girl's brain is wired for connection, it is also wired to create a community where she is at the centre. She walks a fine line between needing to maintain harmony and not be left out of the group whilst remaining at the centre of her world. In practical terms, this means a girl needs to constantly use her negotiation skills to maintain harmony if she wants to keep her friends.

In the early years of primary school, my experience has been that girls tend to form a close bond with just a few other girls. Bossiness is tolerated up to a point, but if one particular girl always has to be in charge of decision making, the others will soon stop playing with her unless she renegotiates the rules. Moving into the middle years of primary school girls continue to play with other girls. They can be totally devastated by a fight with a close friend and also feel miserable if their best friend is absent from school. And the teenage years are just around the corner!

In puberty, a female is biologically designed to become sexually desirable. If you are a woman reading this, you are probably accustomed to the hormonal ups and downs. If you are a man, you have probably experienced and, perhaps been mystified by, the changes in behaviour this hormonal cycle produces! In a nutshell, the oestrogen/progesterone cycle increases our sensitivity to our emotions and the emotions of others, increases our sensitivity to stress, particularly in terms of relationship conflict, and affects confidence levels.

As the mother of a teenage girl you may know, up to a point, how your daughter feels and be able to empathise, but if your cycle in not in sync with your daughter's, there may be a clash. Teenage angst and moments of high drama for a girl include fights with friends, bad hair days, the overnight arrival of a zit, being too fat or too thin, having no breasts or big breasts, a bumpy nose, awful parents who don't understand her, a boy who likes her or who doesn't like her, nothing to wear ...

While sexual desirability is a biological change, a teenage girl's most important relationships continue to be with other females. Your daughter will need to start distancing herself from you at this time and so her relationships with her girlfriends become even more important. I love the phrase that "language is the glue that connects one female to another"[3]. The hours your daughter spends on the phone or computer chatting with her friends may drive you crazy, but remember she is using this time to find her way and reduce stress.

Teenage girls, and adult women, speak on average two to three times more words per day than teenage boys or adult men. Teenage girls get an enormous amount of pleasure out of connecting in this way with other girls and this behaviour continues into adulthood. Just this morning I was walking along our street and a neighbour I have not met previously complained to me about her husband. We had a quick chat about the hopeless nature of men and I continued on my way. I'm not sure that men have such conversations with strangers!

During adolescence personality differences also become more obvious. In Chapter 5 we talked about personality types and the MBTI descriptions of these types. There is a lot of information on the Internet and in books about these differences. While approximately sixty per cent of females have a 'Feeling' preference, that still leaves

---

[3] Brizendine, L., *The Female Brain*, Transworld Publishers, P. 36

a large number of girls who have a preference for using a more logical and analytical approach.

A mother with a sixteen year old daughter was speaking with me and described how upset she felt about the 'bitch' her daughter was. She felt as though she had done something wrong as a mother and she couldn't understand her daughter's behaviour. When she described the language her daughter used with her friends and family, it was clear that she had a preference for 'Thinking'. The daughter had recently told one of her closest friends that she could no longer be a part of a basketball team because she was too short and too slow. In the mother's ('Feeling' preference) mind this was evidence of her daughter being a bitch; in the daughter's ('Thinking' preference) mind this was a logical reason to exclude her friend from the team. Many women with a 'Thinking' preference grow up feeling invalidated by the feedback they receive from others.

Alongside the enormous hormonal changes occurring in a teenager's body, is a process of individuation similar to that of a toddler when she is moving towards independence. There are also changes in the brain and to put it briefly, the part of the brain that makes us behave 'responsibly' is the last to develop. In terms of observable behaviour, you may see:

- Poor ability to prioritize
- Slow processing of information
- Reduced memory
- Poor problem-solving
- Lack of concentration
- More emotional than rational processing of information

- Impulsiveness
- In some cases reduced motor coordination.[4]

Having a teenage daughter can be really scary. Suddenly she doesn't listen to you any more, let alone heed your advice, because after all, you know nothing! You are aware of all the potential dangers but at the same time she wants more independence and is also taking more risks. Like all the stages of her life, your teenage daughter needs your empathy, understanding, help with managing her emotions and importantly, your trust.

If you establish a strong bond with your daughter when she is young, she is more able to manage the roller-coaster teenage years. If she grows up with a sense of security, belonging and acceptance she will be well equipped to negotiate a path through adolescence. If she is accustomed to receiving emotional support from you through your listening and setting of clear boundaries and expectations she may even seek your advice sometimes!

Bearing in mind all the changes that are occurring in your teenage daughter's body, it is likely that she will make some poor decisions. As a parent, it can be really difficult not to feel angry, ashamed, mortified, horrified – by her behaviour. You may feel that others are judging you for your daughter's behaviour, just like those people who glared at you when she was having a tantrum in the supermarket.

It may be useful, if this happens, to try to distance yourself by thinking of your daughter as one of your close friends. If a close female friend came to you because she had done something wrong, would you be more inclined to listen, treat her with respect and try not to judge her?

4 McCarthy S., seminar on Family Systems, Melbourne, 2011

If your daughter comes to you with a problem that she is ashamed of, consider it a compliment that she feels you can help her. Again, while you are surviving the teenage years, support your daughter, manage your own stress levels and learn to ride the waves – they will level out!

In conclusion:

- There are aspects of female hard-wiring that impact on behaviour.

- Each child is an individual with her own specific needs.

- Your daughter needs to receive the message that she is a legitimate person who has the right to be who she is.

- Your daughter wants to be valued and accepted as the unique person she is.

CHAPTER 8: RAISING BOYS

Boys are different from girls no matter which way you look at it. We are not only talking about the basic physiological and hormonal differences that most of us are aware of, but a lot of more pervasive, lesser known, differences.

If you are parents or grandparents of boys then if in reading this book you do nothing else but also read Anthony Rao and Michelle Seaton's book, *The Way of Boys*, we will have achieved an objective. Obviously we are not going to rewrite what Rao has written, but there are certain elements that we find concerning enough to repeat here.

As Rao points out, in our society there exists a very narrow definition of boyhood. As a consequence, the vast majority of children receiving psychiatric referrals are boys. Another disturbing trend is that very young boys are being labelled. Social, cognitive and emotional development is critical in the time between a boy's second and eighth birthdays. We must halt the current trend to diagnose and medicate boys who do not fit the narrow definition. Of course there are a few children who may need a medical intervention, but overall just let boys be boys. As Rao states, the truth is the vast majority of boys don't have a problem.

We live in a society with ready access to information, statistics and data. Whilst this is a good thing we can become too caught up with what is normal, such as:

- How is his weight compared to other babies or children his age?
- What is his height compared to other babies or children his age?
- When do most toddlers start walking?
- When do most toddlers start talking?

The development of social skills varies widely in young boys. The narrow definition of boyhood shows up again when parents, relatives, early learning centre staff, day care staff, kindergarten teachers and child health professionals make an assessment or diagnosis which alarms us enough to seek professional evaluation and/or medication.

So what is a diagnosis? A diagnosis is an assessment where someone fits a category or a label. In Chapter 10 we discuss assessments in detail. However, at this point we want to point out the issue of authority when people make assessments. We do not have to give anyone the unquestionable authority to make assessments. Even if the assessment is by a distinguished specialist in the field we can always get a second or even a third assessment.

The problem with assessments and diagnoses is that we think we are describing something, and we lose sight of the fact that in doing so, we are also creating the very thing we want to avoid. We may end up with an indelible label. What do we mean by this? If I use a very simple example and say I am not good at remembering people's names, I think I am describing a weakness that I have. However, in the process of describing I am also in the process of believing that it will always be so. If someone else said I have a poor memory, then I and others will be looking for examples where I have poor memory. Any evidence that I do not have a poor memory will not be noticed or will be overlooked as me having a good day. A boy who is diagnosed as having Attention Deficit and Hyperactivity Disorder (ADHD), or any other of the many new behavioural diagnoses, will spend the rest of his life believing there is something wrong with him.

In our opinion, and supported by Rao, medication of young children for behavioural issues should be treated with extreme caution. For example as Rao and others point out, Ritalin, which is often prescribed for children that wear the diagnosis of ADHD, has all of us focus better and concentrate harder. A study by Dr Philip Shaw and colleagues at the National Institute of Mental Health indicates that many boys do grow out of ADHD symptoms.

Graeme's Experience

If I look at my own life growing up as a small boy, had I been born half a century later I am sure I would have been indelibly labelled as having ADHD or worse. To explain what I mean let's go back to MBTI. With MBTI preferences, I find it useful to think of it like a gravitational pull towards one way or preference, but we can at times pull away from it.

There is no right, wrong, good or bad with MBTI preferences. However, there are clear biases in society. Statistics indicate there are more people with ESTJ (Extravert, Sensing, Thinking & Judging) preferences in the world than any other. My preferences are ENFP (Extravert, Intuition, Feeling & Perceiving). My only saving grace is that I at least have an Extravert preference!

Introvert/Extravert

Babies are born with this preference and from a very early stage, if you know what you are looking for, you can fairly accurately determine what a baby's preference is.

Recently I observed my grandson with his mum and his mum's friend and her baby. It was clear that my grandson has an extravert preference as he looked to everyone for connection. The other baby did not extend himself outwardly and he needed time and space to interact with others. Neither are right/wrong, good/bad, normal/abnormal. Just different!

Boys with an introverted preference are often labelled as loners because they want to play alone and not interact with other children. "He is not developing normally!" At least sixty per cent of children are extravert and do interact with others in their play. When the boy with an introvert preference is continually pestered by an extraverted preference child who wants to become involved he may, until he learns some better strategies, lash out either physically or verbally at the constant interruptions. Then the labels really start to flow. He is on the autism spectrum, has ADHD or even bipolar disorder! There is nothing wrong with children who have an introvert preference. Just give them their much desired time alone.

If you think you have an introverted boy, perhaps read Marti Olsen Laney's book, *The Hidden Gifts of the Introverted Child*.

Don't force your introvert child to be an extravert, just teach them to be sociable when the need arises. When you meet someone, have your introverted preference child look the person in the eye, say hello, and then let them be.

Writing this book is very much introverted behaviour

and I use Jenny's house at Blairgowrie to minimise the distractions for me. However, to get started after waking up I need some extraversion, so I go out to a cafe for coffee and, most times, breakfast. Then I am okay for a while until I get the pull towards extraversion again so I might go for a walk, a bike ride or go to the shops for a break.

Intuition/Sensing

As someone who was born hard wired to have ENFP preferences and to mature in a certain way, by the time I was about five years old my intuition preference was fully matured. I was creative in all things, and always in la-la land (dreaming). Here is where the trouble can start. A fully developed intuitive preference has, as the opposite, a fully immature sensing preference. So what does this mean? It means that for me, and others who have sensing as least preferred preference, then my hearing, seeing, taste, touch and smell almost fades away. At school – which I hated – I was required to pay attention, to listen and to see, etc. I remember in Prep that there were big pictures of the alphabet at the top of the blackboard. On occasion I was kept in after school to point out the letters as Miss Mill called them out – the detail? – forget it! Nowadays I am sure I would have been diagnosed as ADD!

What about the H – ADHD? Well after being forced to stay in the sensing domain too long I would get a feeling, like a force or energy build up, and I just wanted to get out of there. Even today when I am required to sit in a conference I get the same feeling, but as an adult I will get up and go up the back or leave the room or simply draw something on my pad. So I must have had ADHD!

Feeling/Thinking

But wait, it gets worse for me. I have a feeling preference and it was fully matured at about ten or eleven years of age. I was considered as soft and weak by other boys and as a sensitive kid by parents and teachers. By this stage I was becoming a bit disturbed that there was something wrong with me, especially as the feeling preference has a stronger gravitational-like pull to human values and needs than to the thinking preference, which is about analytical and logical skills. What are we required to do at school? Be logical and analytical! By late primary school I knew something was wrong with me because I could not pay attention to the teacher (I would be paying attention to my creative side), could not be logical and analytical, and got so disturbed at the aggression, discipline and punishment that one teacher was renowned for dishing out to kids that I was put on a nerve tonic!

Perceiving/Judging

I have a perceiving preference which is about having more questions than answers and being open to all kinds of possibilities, and being flexible. I am happiest when my day has no structure and I can allow it to unfold just like my weeks away writing. But school is about structure, start and finish times, class times, play times and lunch times. What is more, it is about having answers and they made us do exams to make sure we knew the answers. Arghhh! No wonder I and my middle son hated school so much. Do I have ADHD? Is there something wrong with me? I certainly felt there was, and I felt invalidated. Have I grown out of it? When I was thirty-five years of age I became a mature age student and went on to become a qualified psychologist and coach. What I didn't know then, but I do know now, is that by the late teens my thinking preference was matured and by my mid-thirties my sensing preference was fully matured (it still disappears often when my intuitional pull takes over). If my ability to fully use my five senses didn't mature until my mid-thirties then I would argue that, without enormous effort and stress, I did not have the aptitude to gain the qualifications I now have, until I reached my mid-thirties.

    I am very happy doing what I do and I don't consider it work in the traditional sense. I am an extravert so my focus is on other people; people because I have a feeling preference which is about people's values and needs. My intuition preference is about how people could be and my perception preference is about having more questions than answers. I am writing this book because I am focused on parents and children, and how they could be.

I have three sons; the eldest one has a doctorate in physiotherapy and works as a physiotherapist along with being involved at a university with research in the same field. He has Introvert, Sensing, Feeling and Judging preferences which are more aligned to his mother.

My middle son, who also has ENFP preferences the same as I do, hated school to the point that his mother wondered at one time if he had ADHD, a question that I immediately convinced her to dismiss. After completing Year Ten he commenced an apprenticeship as a pastry chef, during which time he won the National Baking Championships.

My youngest son is a very successful photographer and with his partner, runs a photography business. We have not as yet established what his preferences might be.

I tell you this regarding raising boys, as we listened to each of them and supported them in whatever they chose to do. All are very happy with what they do.

Alison's experiences

According to Louann Brizendine, author of *The Male Brain*, boys have "... larger male brain circuits for exploratory behaviour, muscular and motor control, spatial skills and rough play."[1]

So what might this look like in a baby boy? My son was very active in utero and this continued! As a newborn baby he didn't like being held a lot and often preferred to be on the floor where he could move his limbs freely. He

---

1 Brizendine, L., *The Male Brain*, Harmony Books, P. 13

loved looking at his mobile and other moving objects. He was walking at ten and a half months and climbed over the garden fence and out into the street before his first birthday.

Some mothers of baby boys have expressed their fear that their son is not connecting with them and doesn't seem to need them in the same way their daughter did at the same age. If we go back to brain wiring, boys' interest in moving objects and shapes is a design feature to help them develop the visual and spatial skills they traditionally needed to be a good hunter.

It can be an exhausting task keeping your toddler son safe, at the same time as allowing him to continue to develop his need to explore the world. Louann Brizendine (*The Male Brain*) makes an interesting point about this. She writes that an expression of fear on a mother's face will probably prevent a girl from pursuing a dangerous act, but a boy of the same age will continue his investigations. It's not that he doesn't understand her expression, but his need to touch, experience and explore new things is a very strong drive. Boys of this age need lots of experiences and the freedom to investigate the physical world for themselves. In my experience sand, water, building blocks and moving toys are great additions to any place where boys play. If you are fortunate enough to have a secure outdoor area, your son can develop his skills through play without you constantly having to protect him from danger!

Happier Parents, Happier Children, Happier World

A note on deliberate misbehaviour

Because boys like to test systems, one of the ways they experiment with this testing process is to see what behaviours provoke interesting responses from adult carers. The quick glance, glint in the eye and expression of glee are giveaways! Having the child stand in the corner is a popular management strategy, but what if he won't stay there and is successfully engaging you in this new game? According to Anthony Rao in *The Way of Boys*, removing a boy to his room – that is equipped with punching pillows – when he is having a tantrum, has several benefits that make sense to me. Firstly, he learns to calm himself down and secondly, as a teenager and adult he will have learnt to walk away from situations and calm down, rather than react aggressively.

As boys develop they continue to learn best through experience. In my experience, boys tend to enjoy hands-on activities where they can use their motor and spatial skills to work things out by trial and error. They also appear to enjoy grouping and categorising objects, so if your pre-school age son develops a liking for colour coding his T-shirts or lining up his socks, don't panic!

Boys' play also tends to be more active than that of girls and often highly competitive. While styles of interaction are also related to a child's natural preferences (see Chapter 5), the biology of the male brain drives boys to want to be bigger, stronger, faster and always first. As a Prep teacher I had to develop strategies to cater for this behaviour, or there was always pushing and shoving to line up first, come in first, go out first and so on.

It amuses me to watch young children in running races. Many boys will give it their all and so will some girls, but there are invariably a few girls who are running with their friends and chatting as they run – or walk. The competitive and physical nature of boys' play is how they develop their social, cognitive and emotional skills. For a more in-depth understanding of boys' development, I recommend reading *The Way of Boys* by Anthony Rao.

What about emotional intelligence and empathy for others? While this is also linked to a child's natural preferences, there are more thinking preference males than females. This often means that empathising with others will not come naturally to many boys.

If you want your son to learn to read feelings, he may need to be taught directly. Lots of talking won't help but boys do understand actions. Anthony Rao writes that empathy is a skill that boys begin to learn after the age of around eight, remembering of course that there are many different paces and pathways in children's development.

A strategy I used successfully as a teacher was to say things like, "I can't concentrate on reading this story while you are talking. I'd like you to stop please." Or, "Sam won't play with you because you're not taking turns. What could you do next time you play this game?"

As often as possible, it is best to let boys sort things out for themselves. I believe if they learn to deal with frustration and solve problems by themselves they will learn to control themselves in different situations and build resilience that will stand them in very good stead for those challenging teenage years.

Teenage Boys

Testosterone! Between the ages of nine and fifteen, there is a twenty-time increase in testosterone levels. Together with increasing vasopressin, the teenage male brain develops "increased sensitivity and growth of sexual-pursuit circuits and territorial aggression" [2]. The increase in these hormones means the early childhood behaviour of competition, exploration and action, will be much stronger.

A testosterone-fuelled brain gives a teenage boy that feeling of invincibility as he distances himself from his parents and becomes an independent adult male. Not only does he need to distance himself from his parents at this time, he also needs to establish himself in the male hierarchy. He needs to fit in with his peers, as it is the feedback that he receives from his peers that lets him know if he's accepted by others.

I was a single mother at the time and can only write about this from a mother's perspective as I have no idea whatsoever what it is like to be a teenage boy.

My lovely son – who by the way is a lovely son again – turned into a non-communicative, door slamming teenager who experimented with all sorts of risky behaviour, of which I probably, and thankfully, know nothing about. He dressed like all the other boys in town, spent most of his time at home in his room and communicated with me using mostly grunts. Thank goodness for competitive sport which he continued to play, as I believe this was a positive influence as he had some positive male role models, a good peer group and a healthy outlet for some of that energy. Thank goodness also for the town grapevine and the support of the parents of my son's friends – together we stand, divided we fall. And thank goodness they grow out of it!

I had a delightful encounter with a teenage boy just yesterday. I was waiting at the tram stop and watching him approaching. His hair was messy and multi-coloured, he

2 Brizendine, L., The Male Brain, Harmony Books, P. xxii

had lots of piercings in his face, one of those big earlobe holes made by a giant earring, an anti-Jesus black hoodie, low-slung jeans and holey shoes. He looked a bit scary. He sat down beside me at the tram stop and said, "Excuse me, do you mind if I smoke, it's just that some people don't like it?" After thanking him for asking, we had a bit of a chat until the tram arrived. I wanted to call up his mother and reassure her that he was going to be okay.

In conclusion:

- We hope that in this chapter we have been able to alert you to the dangers of accepting a narrow definition of normal behaviour.

- If you have a son or daughter who has been marginalised by the assessments of others, it is highly probable that there is nothing wrong with them; they are possibly just a little different from the majority, and as they grow up they will learn to use their lesser preferred preferences when needed.

- We must remember, though, that we cannot change our preferences; we are hard wired that way, but we can change our behaviour when we are "on duty". When we relax we will revert to our natural preferences.

CHAPTER 9: BONDING AND RELATIONSHIPS

So far we have discussed listening, and knowing ourselves and our children. The key to this, as parents, is having an open mind and an investigative nature towards your children, and also encouraging your children to continue with their investigative nature. It would seem that by the third year of school, children begin to lose this, possibly because the nature of many schools is to teach what has been accepted that should be taught and by when, and then check that it has been learnt. This schooling process is most likely the result of the blank slate theory.[1]

In this chapter we want to cover the importance of bonding and relationships, which starts before a child is born and continues to well after you are grandparents.

If we approach babies, toddlers, children and teenagers with a mood of wonder and curiosity, and remember we don't see the world as it is, but how we are, then we will be better able to embrace one another's differences. Even though they are our children, they are all different observers.

1 Lawrence,G. *Finding the Zone*, Prometheus Books, P. 18-20

From a very early age relationships can start to break down and bonding can be impaired. How can this happen? Let us start from the bond between the mother/father and baby. The bond between the baby and his parents can start before the baby is born, if the parents gently massage or rub the baby through the mother's belly, and talk in gentle tones to him. There is plenty of research evidence that new born babies recognize their parents' voices over others. Today, with so much more enlightenment, a new born is placed straight away onto the mother's tummy and the bonding is further enhanced. If the father is present, and thankfully they too are more often than not these days, an early nurse of the baby by the dad also enhances early bonding. If, in the case of an emergency, the chance to bond with the new born is not feasible, all is not lost, and when you do have the chance the baby will still recognize your voices over others. Simply nurse and talk to the baby in gentle, soothing, relaxed tones.

My youngest grandson has been exposed to a wide network of friends and relatives from a very early age and clearly has bonded to a lot of people, as evidenced by his delight when he sees people he knows. He is also comfortable meeting new people, though this is easier for him as he has a preference towards extraversion. He is also very comfortable with his mother leaving him with people while she has time out. He is not anxious that she is not there; he clearly does not suffer from separation anxiety.

In Chapter 6 we talked about taking care of ourselves and our children through stress management, and if you have been doing this before the birth, things will always go better.

I have no doubt that a mother who actively manages her stress levels throughout the pregnancy will be far less likely to suffer from post natal depression. Remember that during birth, both mother and baby have gone through a stressful time, and if they have been managing their stress levels they will be less likely to be dystressed. The less stressed the parents and baby are the greater the bonding will be, and the happier all will be. If the mother is stressed or anxious or misinformed about breast feeding, for example, then tension can begin to arise between the mother and baby, and this can also carry over to tension between the father and mother, and/or father and baby. Likewise as we have mentioned previously, a mother's story about broken sleep can have a detrimental effect. This immediately starts a drift in the bonding and also in what should be a wonderful and happy experience for all.

Even when you are sleepy in the middle of the night it can be a great bonding opportunity. I remember clearly waking up as one of my sons had just finished his feed only to get a beautiful smile from him that would melt anyone's heart.

Pre baby time the husband and wife were the primary relationship, but with a new baby coming into the home a whole new dimension takes place. The new baby is the focus of attention and there is less attention paid to each other. The shared understanding or background of obviousness has been shifted. Suddenly the coordination of action has all changed, the level of love has changed and the stress of it all increases. If the new baby is the second or third then this can also create tension with there now being divided attention between first and second born and mum and dad. The key factor that gets to the very heart of it all is relationships, and the conversations affect the quality of the relationships. When relationships start to break down we do the very reverse of what we could do. What we could do is have conversations about what we are experiencing but what often happens is we withdraw and do not have conversations, and we are less happy.

Newborn babies have very limited ways of communicating to us and even more limited distinctions about the world they have come into. They do not know about time or the future. How could they without well developed language? All they know is when they need some attention such as hunger, thirst, cuddles or discomfort. They may need sounds, as they could hear plenty before they were born. Babies don't want or need structure imposed on them. When they are in need of something, such as milk, they have a basic survival mechanism which says "now". When this is not met they become anxious as they do not know about the future or time, so they don't understand they will get fed in five minutes. They don't understand about waiting.

This also has an impact on bonding and relationships as they become anxious about being away from their mother. They become clingy to the mother for fear that she will not be there when they need her, which limits the bonding opportunities with other members of the extended family. They may develop separation anxiety when they have to be left with someone else. My youngest grandson was fed upon demand and attended to as soon as possible in his early days, and he has no separation anxiety and readily goes to others. He also quite happily stays with others as he has also learnt that his mother will be back when he will need her, or that others will take care of his needs. Once he reached twelve months of age he started to develop his own routine as to when he sleeps and for how long. As mentioned previously in Chapter 3 on listening, it's about listening to your baby and wondering how they might be observing, given who they are.

As I have mentioned before and repeat here, please do not go down the track of feeling guilty about your parenting. You did what you did, given what you knew at the time, and with much love, just like your parents and your parents' parents did. This is about learning that maybe there are better ways and if future generations can learn better ways, then we will have a happier world.

I have spoken about the importance of relationships in life. They are at the core of our lives and family. If the relationships with significant others (husbands, wives, children, in laws etc.) are non-existent, completely broken down, or poor, then conversations either will not happen or they will be of poor quality, and much unhappiness will prevail. In addition, broken down relationships also have negative moods associated with them. We need to manage relationships, not only our own relationships, but to ensure sound relationships around us. This can only be done through truly grasping the notion of different observers and then having in depth conversations.

I used to have an assessment that I had the worst of all mothers-in-law! When I understood the notion of different observers, I understood she was given her own unique hard wiring, her unique upbringing, and her unique life experiences. I went from a negative assessment to really embracing her for who she was, and would genuinely give her a hug and tell her I loved her. Children also learn from observing (as do we all), and if they are exposed to a broken down relationship with a significant other, they will learn that this is also part of life; that it's okay to not be speaking to someone, to have enemies.

We strongly believe bonding is about embracing diversity, understanding we are all different observers and repairing adversity. We advocate it is about having the difficult conversations, sharing each other's observations, and working towards a shared understanding. Many of us shy away from these conversations, often because our attempts just seem to make things worse, but it is a skill that can be mastered.

Public and Private Conversations

A key aspect of mastering awareness, of being mindful rather than mindless, is to listen to our private conversations, the ones that are incessantly going on in our heads. As a psychologist and coach, some of my best coaching, as indicated to me by feedback from my clients, has been from listening to my private conversations. Some might call it listening to your intuition; others might call it trusting your 'gut'. What I observe about myself is that when I do listen to my private conversation and bring some of it forth into a public conversation, it has, more often than not, been extremely useful. Some of my clients have been shocked at the accuracy of my 'what is going on in my head' conversations. Sometimes it has no relevance to what has been discussed but other times is very relevant to the issue being addressed. My clients might say, "Where did you get that from? I have not even mentioned that but it is so true."

Listening to our private conversations leads us to greater depths of mastering awareness, of observing differently and ultimately to mastering our intentions and how we engage in our transformation. Sometimes these private conversations, intuition, gut feelings, are highly relevant to parenting. I think we listen at a very subtle level, maybe even unconsciously, but we could develop the confidence to share these thoughts even if they are not relevant. If, for example, you look at your child and the thought jumps into your mind that they are being bullied at school, where did this thought come from? Did it just jump into your head, or did you listen at some level to something that had you think this way? Remember that in our belief, listening involves the five senses, plus your interpretation.

Sometimes we even have private conversations about our private conversations. Your private conversation about your private conversations might be that I might be wrong and if I share it I will look silly, or something similar. When I share my private conversation I also carefully listen to how the person responds, to what I hear and see, etc. This helps me to assess if I am on the wrong track or maybe on the right track but they are being defensive or are in denial.

In sharing my private conversations I ensure that my finger is always pointing at myself, metaphorically. I preface any of my sharing of my private conversations with something like, "Let me share with you what is going on in my head", or, "I am being distracted by some chatter in my head which I would like to share." If it has no relevance or is not correct then that is okay; it was just chatter going on in my head and when I have shared it I can focus more readily on listening to them. I am very careful to not have the finger pointing at them. That then sounds like I have the truth about them. That then is projecting my opinion onto them. In doing this we would typically be saying "You" as opposed to "I". "I'm wondering if you are happy at school." Not, "You are not happy at school!"

Of course, some of our private conversations about our private conversations must be listened to, as to share all our private thoughts and conversations can be very damaging to others, and/or to us. Sometimes it is best kept to ourselves and maybe even put out of our minds. This is especially so with negative private conversations which are ungrounded and/or getting in the way of being able to relate to a person. True mastery involves knowing the distinction between what to share and what not to share. Ask the key question, "For the sake of what concerns would I share what I am thinking right now?" Another question might be, "What will I take care of if I share what I am thinking right now?"

The Distinction of Breakdowns

I have used the term breakdowns already a number of times and this distinction requires careful explanation because of the commonly held understanding of the term breakdown, being a negative experience and usually of something that stops working. When we use this distinction in the domain of the Ontological interpretation we mean a breakdown of the transparency of the moment, or of the flow of life. As a simple example, I want you to stop reading, move away from where you are and quickly fold your arms. Notice how you fold your arms. Which arm is on top and which is underneath? In our interpretation you did this transparently – you did not need to think about it – it is well practised and from a very early age. Now unfold your arms and fold them the other way, with the arm that was on top now underneath. Notice how hard and uncomfortable it is. This is what we call a breakdown in your transparency of folding your arms.

Breakdowns exist within the individual and are part of the way they are observing. It is not always negative as we commonly believe. For example, in our work we have an interpretation that we help parents address their breakdowns. That is obvious, you say. Isn't that what a lot of coaches and psychologists do? Well yes, but let us take this a bit further. As I sit here writing, a client telephones and requests some assistance with a breakdown. Not only is this a breakdown for them, possibly negative, it is a positive breakdown for me. My transparency in the moment has been broken as well.

Bonding and Relationships

We can also create a breakdown. We have couples who appear to be doing very well as parents, but they call us to enhance their parenting and relationships, knowledge and skills. They created the breakdown to strive to be even better.

What has this got to do with parenting? We claim that most of the way we parent is transparent to us. We do what we do, given who we are and how we were parented ourselves. Breakdowns begin to occur when the father and mother come from families with different upbringings. With these breakdowns we can, through conversations, see the opportunities to transform, but to do this we must remember we are different observers and that we do not hold the truth about it. If we do hold the truth we will have conflict and demand that each obeys the other!

Differing views of parenting not only creates conflict between parents, it can also be very confusing for children. Dad thinks mum lets the kids get away with anything, mum thinks dad is too harsh and strict; they both think their way is right! Apart from the obvious conflict between the parents – and grandparents – the children hear very conflicting messages. I have worked with a family with this dynamic and listened to the frustration expressed by both parents and both sets of grandparents. They never had a conversation about what they saw as important in terms of raising a family; all parties 'knew' their way was the right way and spent a lot of time and energy trying to convince the others that they were right. What did this look like for the child? At pre-school he was diagnosed with a behavioural disorder, which unfortunately made the problem much worse as Mum used that as a reason to explain a great deal of unacceptable behaviour, and Dad became stricter as he thought this was the answer. By the time he got to school, Alan was unable to work or play with any of the other children and quickly earned the reputation of being a bully. The school, and Alan's teachers, provided very consistent boundaries and logical consequences for unacceptable behaviour, had daily conversations with the parents and Alan's behaviour began to improve; he was able to make friends and he was a much happier boy! I believe that if he had more consistent parenting from a young age, many of these problems would have been avoided.

Hopefully, as you read this book we are creating breakdowns of your transparencies about parenting. Having said this we are not claiming we have the truth here either. If we were to do this we would be denying ourselves the opportunity to learn even better ways about this very topic.

When you read how we use the term breakdowns in the context of transparency, what is happening to you? How are you observing this? What are your assessments about this distinction? How might you observe this differently? Are you open to possibilities or are you saying you don't like this use of the term? I will speak more about breakdowns to our transparency in the next chapters.

Emotions as Breakdowns

As we have discussed in Chapter 4, we all have moods and emotions. Emotions occur as a result of some event, external to us or as internal thoughts, feelings or private conversations. We all have emotional reactions, and they occur in all aspects of our lives. To deny them, or not listen to them, is to deny a natural part of life and the opportunities that they might present. In the book, *Destructive Emotions*, narrated by Daniel Goldman, examples of research are cited where even Tibetan monks, who are well practised meditators, are unable to prevent momentary emotional reactions. Much has been written about emotional intelligence and for good reason. In our experience, people continue to suppress or play down emotions and certainly do not talk about them, especially if they cannot apply any logical explanation to them.

On one occasion, I was working with a couple and they seemed to be arriving at a decision point. I observed the man looking somewhat hesitant so I asked what was going on for him. He responded from an emotional perspective that it did not feel right but was embarrassed because he could not offer a logical explanation. However, this was the catalyst for further conversations and the resultant outcome was a different decision. Had the emotional reaction not surfaced, the possibility of a poor or wrong decision was imminent. Using the distinctions that I have introduced to you so far, the emotion was a result of an unidentified breakdown. This emotion then created an additional breakdown for this person, which then led to conversations in which the un-surfaced breakdown was identified; from this breakdown the couple came to a different decision.

The key message is to develop mindfulness of our emotions as breakdowns to our transparency in life, listen to them and, if necessary, seize the opportunity. It could be as simple as, "Did I listen incorrectly to what she said" or, "It could be that I am experiencing something that might be significant to others that I need to share".

Fortunately a lot of our emotions are happy ones. Listen to them and share them with others as well. They too are contagious.

The Bigger the Breakdown, the Bigger the Transformation

If we embrace all breakdowns in our transparency as opportunities, then a whole new world of possibilities shows up for us. When we experience what we assess to be a positive breakdown of our transparency, then it is easy to see opportunities. Inventors have the ability to see breakdowns as opportunities. As a child I lived near a big expensive house. I asked my mother how someone could afford to build such a big new house. The answer was that the owner was the inventor of the safety pin. He saw the breakdown occurring for many and he invented the safety pin.

The challenge is to see the possibilities when in the midst of what we assess to be a big negative breakdown to our transparency. Much of my work as a coaching psychologist is to help clients see the possibilities from their breakdowns. I have seen many people who have lost their jobs for whatever reason. At the time this was a big breakdown for them. Many have since come to the realization that although it appeared disastrous at the time, they were not as happy as they could have been and went on a career correction course and engaged in a big positive transformation. For many, even the concept of work has taken on a new meaning.

Our relationships and our bonding with each other and our children can be seriously impaired by our listening, our observing and the subsequent conversations we do or don't have. Conversely, if you check on your listening and how you are observing, and look at the conversation you could have, then you can enhance bonding and relationships.

Three Types of Conversations

We can work through the breakdowns in our transparency by directly or indirectly dealing with our moods and emotions and by engaging in three types of conversations. I will explain these conversations in detail over the next three chapters.

1.   Conversations for Stories and Assessments

From our work and observations of people in all walks of life, most people engage most of their time in conversations for stories and assessments. In the process of engaging in this type of conversation we think that we are describing how things are. This is an important conversation as it allows us to establish where we are at. However, there is another side. We think we are describing how it is but in the process we lose sight of the other side of the equation; we are not only describing, we are also creating! Let me give you a couple of examples. When a client says to me, "I am a lousy father", they are describing how they believe themselves to be; however, in the process they are also creating the future. They will be recognized by themselves and others as a lousy father. When I had a story and a negative assessment about my mother-in-law I could not see any other way of observing her, and I observed things that reinforced my assessment. I could not see a possibility of improving my relationship with her. In my mind at the time the problem was with her, so my finger was pointing at her! Consequently, my conversations only served to maintain or further distance myself from her.

A different example is an English explorer, John Batman, who stood on the banks of a river in Victoria, Australia, and described what he saw. His words were that this would be a good site for a village. Well over a century later the city of Melbourne is still growing.

The distinction between describing and creating as outcomes of stories and assessments is an important one in coaching parents and children through their breakdowns. Sometimes it is as simple as placing the word "yet" to the end of an assessment. A child may say, "I cannot catch balls." The child could readily see it differently if they understood, "I cannot catch balls yet!" Often they can become 'stuck' in their breakdown because of not seeing this distinction, and that of the possibility of the future being different.

2. **Conversations for Possibilities**

We call these types of conversations 'magic wand conversations'. When I assess that I am clear about my client's breakdown, and I assess my client assesses I am clear about it, I often ask them what it would be like if I could wave a magic wand and everything is just how they would like it to be. If clients are not ready to engage in this type of conversation we may have to directly work on their mood or we may have not fully covered the stories and assessments. When we engage in this type of conversation we not only open up possibilities but we also find a significant shift to a more positive mood. If nothing else this is a great way to have people feel better.

Let us imagine for a moment that we say to the child, "If we could wave a magic wand and you could catch balls, how would that be?" It is insufficient to leave it here though, so we then need to select one of the possibilities we wish to work on, and engage in the third type of conversation. What do we need to do to help the child be able to catch balls? Offer to coach them or help them make requests of others?

3. **Conversations for Coordinating Action**

This type of conversation involves making requests and offers and making and managing commitments. As parents, it is helpful to remind ourselves that the whole world is a network of help just waiting to be tapped into. Make a request! How helpful was it when someone offered to look after your child/children for a time just to give you a break? I will outline all the steps and details of this type of conversation in Chapter 11.

Balancing the level between the types of conversations

The role of parents is to ensure a balance between the three types of conversations. As mentioned previously, we observe that most people engage in stories and assessments most of the time. What we observe happens next is that people either go straight to action by skipping over conversations for possibilities or they become involved with conversations for possibilities but no action. For example, we might have a child who is not performing as well as they could at school (stories and assessments) and we go straight to action. Right, less play time and more homework! We fail to look at all the possibilities. Or we could speculate, and speculate, and speculate about what might be happening and about what might be possible but not take any action. Hmm. Maybe he has ADHD. Maybe he needs to have a different teacher. Maybe she needs to have a tutor. Maybe we should talk to her teacher. Maybe when she grows up it won't be a problem. Unfortunately much of what we observe is that people are so busy 'doing' that they do not take time to interrupt their 'busyness' in order to reflect and speculate about possibilities. With the rate of change (breakdowns) we are all experiencing in all walks of life, we see it as an imperative that we engage in more conversations for possibilities, and to be creative and innovative, rather than jumping to action.

In conclusion:

- Relationships are at the core of family life.

- Good relationships allow us to have good quality conversations.

- Good quality conversations can build and enhance relationships.

- We can look at breakdowns as opportunities.

- We can work through breakdowns using the three different types of conversations.

- During your conversations, remember that you don't see the world as it is; you see the world as you are.

Over the next three chapters we will describe in much more detail how to get the best out of the three types of conversations.

CHAPTER 10: CONVERSATIONS FOR STORIES AND ASSESSMENTS

In Chapter 9 we introduced three different types of conversations. In this and the following two chapters we will go into much more detail about each.

Conversations for stories and assessments help us understand where people are coming from. These conversations are necessary to understand breakdowns, understand how someone is observing things, to relay facts and figures, make assessments etc. When we embrace the interpretation that we don't see the world as it is, only as we observe it, then we will share our assessments differently. For example, you could say, "He is a very shy little boy." However, that is what you are observing given the observer you are, so more correctly you could say, "I find him to be a shy little boy." This creates a space for others to share their observations. I then could say what I observe is an introvert little boy. This allows us to have a conversation to get closer to what might be so. If you say "he is", it assumes it is the truth and if I challenge your assessments you may want to more rigorously defend your statement. This potentially shuts down conversations. Conversations for stories and assessments enable us to gain common understanding.

However, as mentioned previously, this type of conversation has a flip side. We not only describe how things are, we potentially create how things are or could be. Also when we engage in this type of conversation it gives us an excuse – often transparently – to continue the way we are. Only this morning I heard a lady say, in response to her daughter saying she needs to get a new mobile phone, "Oh I am no good with new technology." She now has an excuse for not getting one and for not learning new technology. As parents, we invite you to be ever mindful of the excuses you might have about yourself and/or might be conveying to your children. Excuses can shut down possibilities.

As mentioned previously, Bruce Lipton in his book, *The Biology of Belief,* states that the messages children receive, especially up to the age of six, have a profound influence on their developing brains.

From conception to the age of six, children are processing a huge amount of information. Alongside physical skills, children are learning beliefs, attitudes and behaviours and transferring this information into the subconscious mind to free up more space in the conscious mind for more learning. Both positive and negative messages are heard and retained as 'truths'. Many of us have probably struggled to change some ingrained, negative beliefs we hold about ourselves.

Most people engage in this type of conversation for a disproportionate amount of time compared with the other two types. In our work with parents we observe the almost incessant negative stories and assessments that are being engaged in by family members and friends. This seems to be the topic of most of their conversations. What we don't hear a lot of, are conversations for what might be possible, nor conversations for coordinating action to improve or change things, or to move towards a better way of behaving.

What we are describing also has a significant impact on our emotions and moods. For example, if we had just won a free holiday for all the family our mood in describing this could be significantly different than if we were describing some form of crisis, or how much we dislike our neighbour.

Language Creates Reality

When we engage in descriptive conversations we think we are describing something, but we are also creating reality and potentially locking ourselves into the future being a certain way. When I was first exposed to the Ontological interpretations at a conference in San Francisco in 1994, I was so impressed I stood up in front of nearly 100 people and said that I was going to take this work to Australia. Little did I know what I was creating when I did this, but I very rapidly started to realize when I was in Boston later that year with the same group of fellow students; a number of them came up to me and inquired how I was going with taking this work to Australia! I had already created a reality, an action that now has a life of its own. There are now many people in Australia who are teaching the Ontological interpretations, and the numbers of people who are familiar with the distinctions are growing rapidly.

Most young children are creative and unafraid to

take risks. Sadly, our language takes this away from them all too soon. Most young children know they can dance, draw, read and write and they begin formal learning with this wonderful confidence and willingness to have a go at anything. With our education system's current focus and value placed on numeracy and literacy standards, it won't be long before this willingness to explore disappears.

> Let me, Alison, tell you about Eliza. She is friendly, outgoing and helpful and came to school just over twelve months ago as a highly confident five year old. According to the expected standards, she is a low-achieving, 'at risk' student – already! But that's not the whole story of Eliza. She is creative and invents stories that are much more interesting than the words on the page, but she's learnt that that's not reading. Now she won't read because she knows she can't and she thinks she's dumb. Yes, Eliza needs to learn to read the words on the page, but if our system valued her social skills and creativity, perhaps the impact of her inability to read – yet – would not have had such a negative impact on her story about herself.

When we engage in descriptive conversations we think we are describing something, but we are also creating reality and potentially locking ourselves into the future being a certain way. On my way back from my walk today I caught myself saying, "Not another steep pinch over another sand dune", then I said to myself, "Hey I am just getting warmed up." Then instead of grinding my way over I did it easily.

Let me give you another example. If a parent or child says, "I am hopeless at catching balls", once again we think we are describing how things are, and overlook how we are creating the future.

We cannot over emphasise this important distinction. Too often in our daily conversations we lock ourselves into thinking this is the way it is, and we miss the positive opportunities language can open up.

When we engage in conversations for stories and assessments about people it changes nothing other than to reinforce our story and assessment, and often we engage in these conversations to have someone agree with us! Suppose a parent shares with us that their child is very shy. Not only will they continue to notice shy behaviour but so, too, will others who buy this story. Any behaviour that suggests not shy will either go unnoticed or dismissed as a bit of aberrant behaviour. If the child hears this story often enough they too will buy the story.

What if we simply observed a child who has an Introvert preference as per MBTI? What we would then observe is a child who prefers to play alone or with maybe only one other child. That child's reactions to their space being invaded takes on a whole new meaning.

From my observation, too many people spend too much time focusing on their weaknesses and on their children's and others weaknesses, rather than on developing their strengths. Focusing only on weakness creates negative moods as well as creating the future.

When people say they are poor parents, they will continue to approach parenting in a certain mood and will limit themselves for what could be possible. Unfortunately this often carries over to the way we bring up our children. We focus on the weaknesses with the negative moods that go with it. "Don't do that." "Stop that." "How could you be so stupid?" Or we might say, "He is a slow developer." "She is not good at reading." "You *are* a naughty boy!"

My grandson, who is currently twenty months old, could be observed at times as being naughty, but I wonder if he is practising his throwing skills and/or testing the boundaries. When his parents stop him doing something, or take a toy from him, they replace it with something else. Sometimes small children in this situation will cry and we interpret this as them wanting the thing that has been taken from them (which may be so), or it might be frustration with the void that is left. My grandson usually seems happy to be distracted from what he was doing and goes on to the next thing.

Many negative assessments can create a reality in a certain mood, and part of the resultant reality becomes further weaknesses such as low self esteem, low self confidence and for some, a sense of unworthiness. An alternative is to focus on what could possibly be achieved. To do this requires us to engage in *conversations for possibilities* and *conversations for action*. I will explore these types of conversations more in Chapters 10 and 11. Good parenting is about managing these conversations and moods and discovering, developing and celebrating what's different about each member of the family.

Language Reveals but also can Conceal

Not only do descriptive conversations describe and create, they can also conceal. When we think we have answers we most often do not have questions. If we observe a crying baby and say, "Oh she is tired", then this seems to be so and potentially closes down any further assessments. If we say, "I think she is tired", we can look for the evidence that this may be so or evidence she might be thirsty, hungry or wet.

We all understand that when we drop something it falls to the ground. The explanation we have is that this happens because of gravity. In the absence of any other explanation we accept that this is so. It might be just possible that having the explanation conceals us from seeing some other possible reason. In the world of physics, what we once accepted as being so is now showing up as not so. In my coaching, my clients often find it helpful to separate the phenomena from the story we attach to it. With my example, the phenomena are that things drop to the ground. The story or explanation is that it is gravity. Many people can become stuck in their story about the phenomena and in doing so this limits them from seeing things differently.

Children who don't fit in with the current norms will often be 'labelled'. As parents we often get some relief from the label: "Ah, that's what is wrong with him." Many parents relax with the thought they now know the answer!

If we use ADHD as an example, once we have the diagnosis a number of things will follow:

1. This label will now be shared amongst family, friends, childcare centre staff and school teachers.
2. This label will be shared with the child who will come to accept, "There is something wrong with me!"
3. This label will be constantly reinforced by the daily routine of taking Ritalin. (Remember that anyone who takes Ritalin will have their attention increased).
4. There may no longer be any questions about the child's needs.
5. The label and the medication will potentially stay for the life of the person.

In Chapter 5 we introduced you to the MBTI and you may find it useful to refer back to this as I discuss the following example.

I, Graeme, have MBTI preferences of Extravert, Intuitive, Feeling and Perceptive (ENFP) as I mentioned in Chapter 4. I was born with the hard wiring to mature in a certain way and to have these preferences for making sense of the world. My least preferred preference is Sensing (using the five senses for making sense of the world). My dominant preference is Intuition. So at school I can distinctly remember *not paying attention* to the teachers or to what was going on! But I was paying attention to my thoughts and imagination, and later on, I and one of my friends sat up the back constantly drawing cars of the

Conversations for Stories and Assessments

future! What is more, if I am forced to pay attention for long periods of time, I, to this day, have an internal (negative?) energy build up that causes me to need to be active or move (hyperactive?). As a mature adult, when in a conference etc., I can give myself permission to wander off in my mind, stand up and go to the back of the room, or maybe go to the rest room. So do I have ADHD? No, I am hardwired to be the person that I am and my investigative nature will take me to different places than others. I suggest that had the label ADHD been around when I was at school, there would have been a high probability that I would have been diagnosed as having it. I already had concerns that maybe there was something wrong with me.

So please stay with an investigative mind, have questions rather than answers, and remember we are all different observers.

Assertions and Assessments are further distinctions that we want to introduce, both of which are part of descriptive conversations. Without these distinctions we can limit what is possible for ourselves and others. We cannot intervene in a world we cannot see.

If we take the following two statements as describing reality, "John is tall for his age" and, "John is 1.2 meters tall", we can fall for the trap of *thinking* that both are the same kind of statement. They look and sound the same. However, a fundamental distinction needs to be made between these two kinds of statements. The distinction becomes apparent if we look at what different social actions the speakers are committing themselves to.

Assertions describe how things are

The language of assertions describes how things already exist in the world. The world leads and the words follow. It is the language of facts. John is 1.2m tall is a fact. We can have John stand against the wall and measure him. Evidence can be produced to establish this to be true.

Many people ask me at this point, "Why not just call them facts?" Facts are true assertions. However, we have two other types of assertions. We can have false assertions which, of course, are not facts. We also can have pending assertions. The weather forecasts are pending assertions. The local forecast for today was that the temperature would be 31 degrees. This was a pending assertion. Now at five p.m. we can say it was a false assertion as the true assertion is the maximum was 33.7. When we make assertions we are committed to providing the evidence if requested.

Assertions also exist in a space of what is agreed to within that community and at a particular time. For example, if I were to speak of a top temperature I would need to be clear if it was Celsius or Fahrenheit. In Australia, the temperature was measured in Fahrenheit until changed to Celsius, so we can say that what is considered true at a point in time can change. An assertion is always an assertion within, and for, an existing community at a point in time.

Assessments are a different form of statement requiring a different social action.

Assessments are a form of declaration, but not every declaration is an assessment. Declarations are very different from assertions. When we make declarations, the words lead and the world follows. Look at how Melbourne is growing following the words of John Batman. When I say, "John is tall for his age", I am making an assessment.

If we did not have language, then the reality that assessments generate would not exist. Assessments do not describe anything that existed before they were made. The reality lives in the interpretation they provide. An assessment always lives in the person who makes it, the observer they are. When a person makes an assessment, it will often tell us more about the person making the assessment than what is being assessed.

I will explain this in greater depth further on in this chapter when I discuss grounding assessments.

Many declarations can be made because of the authority we grant ourselves or others to make them. When we go to the doctor we might grant her the authority to make the assessment of what we have and to declare what medication is necessary. However, if I, as a coaching psychologist, were to make the assessment about your physical health, you most likely would not give me the authority. Assessments as a form of declaration are either valid or invalid, depending on the authority we grant ourselves or others. In my observation, often people give others the authority when maybe they could question the validity of their assessment.

Much of the hurt we experience is from our loved ones making assessments, because we unquestionably give them the authority. This is not to say we should go through life not giving anyone the authority, but at times it might be useful to question the validity and/or seek to ground the assessment (see below). A person's authority to make declarations and assessments also comes from the role that they occupy in society or in an organization. Their declarations and assessments have validity because of the authority that is inherent in the role they occupy. When we ask young people and adults, "When is a goal a goal?" they usually answer, "When the ball goes through the goal posts". This is incorrect as it is not a goal until the umpire declares it so.

As human beings we are always making assessments. We cannot go through life without assessing people and things. As you read this book you are making assessments.

Not only are assessments valid or invalid, they are also grounded or ungrounded. By grounding I mean that there is evidence (true assertions or facts) to support or not support my assessment. With the assessment that John is tall for his age, what am I doing? To start, I am making a declaration or verdict about John in this moment. Assessments contribute significantly, both positively and negatively, to people's identity. (Assessments are not only about people. Our assessments impact on the identity of products, companies, cultures, countries etc.)

Next, I am making the assessment based on what I have observed in the past. I observed how people, teachers, other parents etc. have responded to John. If you were to ask if I observed John as tall for his age and I say, "No", then you may become suspicious of my intentions and of my assessment. Not only will my authority be questioned, but you could question the validity as to what facts I have to support my assessment.

Assessments do not ground assessments. The grounding must come from something that can be measured. I cannot ground the assessment by saying that Peter said John was tall for his age. I could ground it, however, if I looked at statistics of the average height of boys of John's age. What is measurable is the number of boys and their height as represented in the statistics. Whenever we make an assessment there is an expectation that we can ground our assessment.

Finally, in making assessments I am making predictions about the future. We would not be making assessments if we were not concerned with the future, and we make them because we have learnt that the past can give us some indication about the future. However, when we make assessments, we make the assumption that the past is a good adviser of the future. Because John is tall for his age does not necessarily mean he will be a tall man when he stops growing!

We can navigate our way into the future knowing what we can expect and restricting some possible actions. Based on our assessments we will continue to form certain relationships and avoid others. However, what happened in the past does not necessarily mean it will happen in the future.

I was inattentive at school so certain predictions could have been made about the future for me. I left school after failing Year 11 and yet I am now a qualified psychologist.

We must be open to questioning our assessments about each other and our children. We must stop and question how we are observing people and things and see if we could observe things differently. Our assessments and our assumptions must be open to be questioned and disproved – they must be under constant revision.

I quote Rafael Echeverria from a paper he wrote in 1993 when he was part of The Newfield Group:

> "... people who are generally committed to shaping the future, know how to take full advantage of assessments and guide themselves through the uncertainties of the times to come. At the same time, they must avoid being captives of their assessments, or of the past these assessments bring with them. They must accept that new actions can be produced."

If we fail to see the distinction between assertions and assessments then we may see them all as assertions. When we do this we are limiting our possibilities. For example, if we say, "Graeme is not good at school," and we deal with this as an assertion – as a fact – then we may not see that being a poor student is not a fixed property of Graeme, but a declaration we make based on his past performance. We may project this into the future and assume this is the way Graeme is and will always be. With the use of the three conversations that we offer, Graeme had the opportunity to have a different outcome.

The other concern here is that we don't see the connection between assessments and action. We don't see that if we change the actions we need to change the assessments.

Mary and her parents shared an assessment that she was a very shy young girl, an assessment not shared by her drama class teacher. The teacher worked with Mary to have her take a leading role in the school theatre production. The show, and Mary, was an outstanding success. Suddenly the assessment held by many that Mary is shy seemed silly! Many highly successful actors are introverts.

Grounding Assessments

Grounding Assessments is a procedure to test whether there is evidence to support our assessments; to check whether or not we are standing on solid ground. If our assessments are grounded, then we are better positioned to take care of the future.

In our interpretation there are five steps to grounding assessments. These five steps are also a critical part of assessing children's behaviour. As I have said previously, we make assessments because of our concerns for the future, so we need to be clear about the following:

1. **For the sake of what do we make the assessment?**

   That is, what (concerns) are we taking care of by making the assessment? According to our assessment some things are possible and others are not. If I assess a certain restaurant is dirty then my assessment is for the sake of my health and the health of my family and friends. When someone makes an assessment of me, I find it useful to establish for the sake of what are they making this assessment? Sometimes couples in relationships use assessments to 'push the other's buttons' or raise an assessment which they know will create some tension. When two people come together, one from a very tactile family, the other from a less tactile one, the level of intimacy can become overpowering for the one from the less tactile upbringing. So they use an assessment to create a tension that then puts the emotional distance out a bit. It is less clear what the 'for the sake of' in this situation is. Is it the level of intimacy in the future, or for reducing the likelihood of being hurt in the future? Sometimes in the mood of wonder it can produce a quite intimate and illuminating conversation to inquire as to why this assessment is important to them.

In a family sibling setting the, 'for the sake of what' can also be as obscure. In a competitive family environment one sibling may well make negative assessments about the other in order to gain a competitive advantage, or even in the belief that putting the other down will somehow boost their own self esteem.

The, 'for the sake of what' is not always clear and you may need to question this on some occasions when assessments are being offered.

2. **What (and whose) standards are we applying?**

This is particularly important when assessments are made about our children or our parenting! With children, if we go back to the MBTI, the standard applied for school room attention and behaviour now comes into question. Does the standard serve all children well or just the majority? Is the blank slate theory an acceptable standard today? Or should we continue to encourage the investigative nature of all children?

Previously we introduced you to the Human Synergistics distinctions because we wanted to show you that we will most likely parent our children with similar styles to the way we were parented. When two people come together and have children, potentially there will be a marriage of two different styles of parenting. The key to successful parenting is to come to some agreement about the standards and style. Hopefully you might both be motivated to move towards a constructive style. Be warned though, the extended family (grandparents) and friends will want to offer different standards.

A final note about agreed standards, if you and your partner have not come to an agreement about standards of behaviour expected from your children, then your children may well detect this and play one of you against the other. My son and daughter-in-law recently had a conversation with myself and my wife with a request that we all adopt the same expectation of behaviour with our grandson. We readily agreed to the request but also know the agreed standard will have to be a continual conversation. We will talk more about this in Chapter 12.

3. **In what domain are we making the assessment?**

In our work as parent coaches we repeatedly hear assessments being made about children that are so broad and all encompassing that they potentially damage the children's self esteem and self confidence. Because they are so broad they offer very little in terms of previous steps 1 and 2.

"I cannot trust Kate." Really! Does she steal things? Does she tell lies? Far too broad an assessment!

"I cannot trust Kate to cross the busy roads yet! The other day she ran across the road to see her friend and didn't check for traffic." Ah ha. At this time I now understand exactly in what domain we cannot trust Kate.

In our assessments in life we must be precise with our language and our assessments.

4. **Assertions that support the assessment**

Grounding the assessment is achieved by providing assertions about what we are assessing. If we cannot provide assertions we cannot ground our assessment. We cannot ground our assessments with further assessments, nor with false or pending assertions. When asked why we say, "David is a good father", and we reply, "He is always happy with his kids and he does lots of good things with them", all we have done is replace assessments with assessments. If we were able to reply, "He spends at least two hours each day playing with them and he has read twelve books to them", then the assertions that can be measured are two hours each day and twelve books.

Some assessments may need more assertions to ground them than others. If we pick on poor little Kate again whom we can't trust, and say we can't trust her to tidy her room because in the last month she said she would and yet has not done so, then we would consider that insufficient evidence. If we were to assess that she has agreed to tidy her room every month and yet she has not tidied her room for four months of this year then we might say that could be more grounded.

5. **Assertions that support the opposite assessment**

The number of assertions we can provide does not necessarily mean we can consider it a well grounded assessment. We may have considerably more assertions that could ground the opposite. We could have a situation where we assess that Kate cannot be trusted to tidy her room as evidenced by it not being done for four months of this year. Yet if we look for evidence that grounds the opposite, that Kate can be trusted to tidy her room, we might find that she has done so eight out of the last twelve months.

We also have to consider the weight of evidence we are using to ground an assessment. We may have an assessment that Kate can be trusted to cross the busy road, grounded by she has done so under observation twice a day for the last 100 days. The only grounding for the opposite is twice recently she ran onto the road without looking! Which evidence will we place more weight on?

Unfortunately, we see all too often a parent berating a child for an assessment of poor performance without looking to see evidence for grounding the opposite. If John is bringing you a drink and he drops it, chances are he is going to be already upset without you berating him, plus what about all the times he has brought you a drink without dropping or spilling it? These five steps, if adhered to, provide us with some of the rigor required to be constructive parents and carers.

The Traps of Conversations for Stories and Assessments

As mentioned previously, most people engage in this type of conversation most of the time. What might seem to be idle chatter is not an innocent act. If we accept that language not only describes but also creates reality, that it not only reveals, it can conceal, then it is incumbent on us to manage the descriptive conversations that are occurring, in order to minimize the destruction of the identity of people. This can be done through knowing the distinction between assertions and assessments, managing the assertions and assessments, testing the untested assumptions and grounding the assessments. In addition, descriptive conversations can either enhance our moods or drag our moods down. No more talk about the mother-in-law!

Confusing Knowing with Having an Opinion

Much controversy exists as to whether we should give children a light smack to discipline them and when I listen to the debates I begin to think about what it is that many are doing. I listen to people confusing assertions with assessments, making false assertions and ungrounded assessments. To sum up, I listen to them confusing *knowing* with *having an opinion*. What I find I need to listen to very carefully is what are assertion and assessments, what are true or false, and what assertions (evidence) if any, are there to ground their assessments. Are their assessments valid and do I give them the authority? We must have our radar up to listen for knowing versus having an opinion.

Human Suffering and the Role of Stories and Assessments

We observe that the possession of language alone will produce suffering, and that processes underlying language will compound the suffering. If we suffer physiological pain we immediately assign some story to it. We may also become concerned regarding our own mortality, whereas animals most likely do not know about their own mortality and therefore may not worry as much about the pain they are suffering. In the words of Eckhart Tolle, they live in the space of 'now', not the past or the future.

When we are on the receiving end of negative assessments, it is extremely important to consider all five steps of grounding an assessment. If we consider the feedback to be grounded then we may choose to do something about it. However, if the feedback is related to how we are hardwired then we may not be able to maintain a change in behaviour all the time.

If we find that the feedback is ungrounded and cannot be grounded, then it is invalid and we are wise not to give the person the authority to make the assessment. It is not helpful to relationships to publicly declare we do not give them the authority as this does not take care of the other person. The most useful thing is to let it go past you like the breeze rather than let it disturb and hurt you. This requires practise, especially the more significant the person is to you. You may want to consider for the sake of what was this assessment made and what is this person telling you about themselves? One response you could make to take care of the relationship is to acknowledge that you do understand how they might see it that way. You are not agreeing with them but legitimately acknowledging them as a different observer to you. If you can develop this within yourself then you can also coach your children to be able to protect themselves from psychological harm.

A considerable amount of our coaching of individuals is with people who are suffering psychologically. They come for coaching (and/or counselling) because they are unhappy about themselves. Without wanting to over simplify what are often very serious problems for the clients, the trouble often starts with a significant dose of negative assessments made by themselves and/or others, most of which are ungrounded. Low self esteem and a lot of low self confidence has a strong underpinning of negative self assessments or stories that people hold about themselves or others.

Often what happens when we develop a negative assessment about ourselves or others is that we notice all the evidence that might support our assessment but fail to notice evidence for the opposite. If we do see evidence for the opposite we might say it was a fluke or that she/he is having a good day. Often with our coaching, the individual might be changing their behaviour but others' perceptions of them are not. One relapse over a twelve month period and it is noticed. "Ah, there you go! Leopards don't change their spots!"

I worked with a man who wanted to manage his anger. We were making great progress until one day after several months of being at peace with himself and the world, he returned home after a stressful day at work, tripped over a bike at the front door, and he was momentarily angry. With this his wife declared, "There you go again! Always angry! Can't help yourself, can you?" Then he had to work really hard at regaining his composure!

In conclusion:

- Conversations for stories and assessments are necessary to describe a situation as we see it. However, we must emphasize the potential dark side of these conversations. They can create negative moods and emotions, lock us into the future and drag our perceptions of ourselves and others down.

- A key role of parents is to listen to and manage the conversations for stories and assessments, to be aware that, not only do they describe, but they can create or at least perpetuate the status quo, and that language can reveal or conceal us from the world.

- We must be able to make the distinction between assertions and assessments, and actively seek to ground assessments. When considering others' input and making decisions, it is critical to be able to listen to the distinction between knowing and having an opinion.

- Finally, understand that human beings are in possession of language and much of our suffering is generated in language. If this is so, we can help individuals to question their story about it, question the way they are observing, maybe see it differently and develop a different story about it.

Some of our work involves relationship breakdowns through conflict. Almost invariably both parties experience the same phenomena, but both parties assign different stories to the phenomena and these stories become the truth for them.

We are all different observers and we don't see it as it is, only as we see it. The key for much of the resolution of the conflict involves what we have outlined in this chapter.

CHAPTER 11: CONVERSATIONS FOR POSSIBILITIES

In the previous chapter we looked at the intricacies of conversations for stories and assessments and how they have an impact on our moods. In our coaching we always like to try and engage in some form of what we call 'magic wand' or possibilities conversation at least at the end of each coaching session. This is because it is generally not possible to stay in a negative mood when thinking about how things could be if I could wave my magic wand. It may take a number of sessions to unpack the client's story and for us to be able to understand the breakdown, but if they leave feeling a little better then we have achieved something. However, if the client or the person you are conversing with is not ready to even think about possibilities you may find you might have to let it pass and come back to it.

Conversations for possibilities can be used to help your child or an individual become unstuck from descriptive conversations and they are very good for shifting moods. It is far more helpful to engage your children in conversations for possibilities than sitting down and solving the problem for them. Conversations for possibilities are about what we want to move towards, not what we are wanting to move away from. For parents, if we could wave a magic wand for you right now what would it now look like? It is about moving away from "can't" do it towards "can" do it!

Conversations for possibilities with children can range from very informal relaxed chats while walking the dog to sitting down with them at home. These conversations are very constructive and achievement oriented.

I will now outline a process which has some elements that can be equally as effective when applied to informal chats as to more organized conversations such as solving a problem.

Make a Commitment to Engage in a Conversation for Possibilities

To make a commitment to engage in a conversation for possibilities is often not as easy as it first appears. If it is with your partner they may not want to agree to talk about a situation, depending on how you approach it. With children who for example are getting distressed about homework or an assignment, it might be as simple as sitting down with them to find out what their story is and then invite them to imagine what it might be like when it is all finished and what that might look and feel like?

Interrupt Your Busyness to Find the Time

If I, Graeme, could have my time again as a father, I would think very carefully about saying, "I have not got time." I might have been busy doing something but what I am implying is that what I am doing is more important than you. What is more important than your partner and your children?

If the breakdown involves you and your partner it is often useful to interrupt this cycle, interrupt our 'busyness' and observe what role you are playing in the breakdown. As discussed previously in Chapter 3 we can stand back and observe how we are observing the situation. The breakdown is not a breakdown without someone observing it and declaring it so.

Now this in itself is insufficient. In the act of observing we could observe what mood is present as well. Is it resignation? "Nothing I can do will make any difference." Is it a mood of resentment? "It is your fault!"

In addition, what role is the body playing in this situation? This is not only body language but also the mood shaping the body. People who are caught in moods of resignation and resentment are caught in certain body shapes. Both will possibly complain of neck and shoulder pain because their head is maybe forward of their torso. The observer I am feels negative vibrations from other people and this can impact significantly upon relationships!

As a little exercise, observe someone's body posture and then discretely put your own body into this posture and notice what mood shows up for you.

So what do we need to do to gain a commitment to engage in a conversation for possibilities? One option might be that we need to shift the mood first.

In our relationships with our partners and children we often allow ourselves to be in inappropriate moods and these moods are highly contagious to our partners and our children. It is often helpful to kindle a mood of possibility and ambition as opposed to resignation, and acceptance as opposed to resentment.

Find a Place that is Conducive to Having Conversations for Possibilities Without Interruptions

So what sort of place is conducive to having conversations for possibilities? The ideal place is somewhere where we can be away from the normal distractions of life, both work and home. Somewhere where we can clear our heads and be free to speculate. Interruptions from people coming in, telephones, including mobiles, pagers etc., all distract us from possibilities and drag as back to the very 'busyness' that we are trying to break out of. Maybe have your partner keep the other children out of the room, or maybe go for a walk if you are conversing with one of the children. For older children, maybe take them out for a bite to eat. If you want to connect with your partner, maybe take a weekend away without children. I am writing this book from my friends' beach house as it provides me with this very context.

The Role of the Body

Whenever we are unhappy we invariably change our posture to be looking down. I am unsure but I think it was one of my parents who taught me that I will not find the answers down there. The answers are more likely to come from looking upwards. As a consequence, I encourage people who are about to engage in a conversation for possibilities to master the art of lying down in an upright chair. At least put the hands behind the head and look up. Even lying down on your back has you looking up; maybe in banana lounges beside each other. In this position you are more likely to be in the mood to speculate about possibilities. Our bodies and our moods are intricately connected.

Shift Your Mood to One that is Going to be Conducive to Speculative Conversations

The selection of the venue will have an impact on the mood of the conversation. Places with nice views of the sea or the countryside both impact positively on my mood. There is added value in going on nice walks. Exercise such as walking can positively shift moods. I would suggest think beyond the square. Maybe take a break and go for a walk together. Set up the room to be more conducive or go to another room. Too often we feel constrained by the layout of the room. Often sitting around an open fire is a good place for a speculative conversation. I once heard of a psychologist who works with couples who has them stay in cottages and they sit around the fire and talk.

As mentioned previously, we can only proceed when we feel ready to move on from conversations for stories and assessments. To shift the mood we might need to do whatever we need to do to declare the past complete – to move on from the past. If there has been an imbalance of negative events or stories it is often very helpful to shift the mood by reflecting on what it is we do well.

Here in Australia we are exceptionally good at identifying what we don't do well – it is ingrained in our culture. What we don't do well is celebrate enough of our successes. I find I will always get a list of what is wrong or done badly that is many times longer than a list of what is right or done well. So acknowledge what your sons or daughters or partners do well.

Other more subtle, but nonetheless effective, methods for shifting moods are music, dance, and laughter. Most people play music to suit the mood they are in. I suggest that they play music to suit the mood they want to be in. Music is one of the strongest stimulants to our moods and emotions and, after many years as a musician, I am acutely aware that it does not matter what mood I am in at the start of a gig, I am always in a very positive mood at the end.

Finally, deep relaxation exercises, meditation, yoga etc. all contribute to shifting to a mood of speculation, plus these techniques can free our mind for ideas to come flooding in. I have had many an inspiration come to me while meditating.

Why not introduce some of these techniques at home? Maybe put aside your assessments of your children's music and have them put on music that always makes them feel happy. They may resist initially but they will find it hard to continue to do so.

Much has now been written about EQ or emotional intelligence. We claim it is the role of parents to manage their own and others' moods and emotions. This is not to say ignore all those negative moods and emotions, but to be mindful of them, manage them, reflect on them and ascertain what is driving them. Unfortunately we see many young adults who have deep seated resentment about their parent(s). This resentment usually indicates insufficient conversations over time.

Be Clear What it is You are Speculating About

It could be as simple as having some homework finished to as complicated as having a better relationship or a bigger house or a trip overseas. It is usually helpful to add a timeframe to the magic wand question. It might be next week, two years, for others – five years, and for some it might be comfortable to be open ended. We can start being open ended and then when we move into developing action plans we can decide what is realistic for what timeframes.

Some find it helpful to describe it as though we have actually got there. For example, we might start off by agreeing that it is the date two years from now and then describe how they visualize it to be, then back track and tell the story about how we got there.

With your child it might be to imagine that it is two weeks from now and this assignment is all completed and they have a top mark. Now they should imagine what steps they might have taken to get there. Where did they get the information? Who helped them? What else was helpful? Of all the possibilities, which one do they imagine they chose? How did they do it? Why do they imagine they were successful?

Suspend Some Conversations

Initially, for speculative conversations or conversations for possibilities to be most effective it is helpful to suspend conversations for stories and assessments. This is not dissimilar to the rules of brain storming. For example, it is useful to suspend:

1. **Assessments**

    We have a natural predisposition to be continually making assessments. In conversations for possibilities this has the effect of shutting down the very mood and conversation we are trying to have. Participate with the thought that anything is a possibility. We can come back to your assessments and to what we will or won't use. (There is no, "I can't do it!")

2. **Coherences**

    Again we have a natural predisposition to reject anything that shows up as incoherent. Just accept anything as possible at this stage.

3. **Consistency**

    Ideas and thoughts do not have to be consistent with what we think and know. Just accept them for what they are; a thought or an idea.

4. **Grounding of ideas**

    What we believe we know as facts can often blind us to what might be possible. Accept the contribution for what it is.

I have a story about speculative conversations that I have been telling for so long that I am unsure of its origin. I like the story so much that I also included it in my book on Leadership. If any person knows the source I would welcome the information so I can assign the appropriate credit. However I think it is a good story to demonstrate speculative conversations. It goes like this:

> *There is a large dam somewhere in Europe where high voltage cables are suspended from two towers on the mountains on each side of the dam. The cables are long and go down towards the water before going up to the opposite tower. During certain times of the year ice forms on the cables and creates the potential for them to break. This only happens in the early morning and not when it is windy. During a speculative conversation someone said to install a big fan. The rules were applied and this thought was dutifully recorded. The outcome was others built on this idea and listened for possibilities. A helicopter was utilized to inspect the transmission lines on a daily basis. In conjunction with weather forecasters, the helicopter was scheduled at the appropriate time on days where this ice was likely to form, to fly back and forth a couple of times over the suspended cables. The story has it that this was an effective low cost strategy to overcome the problem. Our normal reaction would have been to reject the idea of having a big fan blowing across from one mountain to the other.*

Build on Ideas

As with brainstorming, the effectiveness of these conversations also involves a commitment to build on others' ideas. In the above example, I doubt it would have been possible to arrive at that outcome without the commitment to build on the ideas of others. Out of all the possibilities decide which ones you would like to progress and when.

This is the step where we decide on what is feasible, what actions we can take now, and what actions can be addressed in the future.

If this is how we see it could be, I wonder what possible conversations and actions we might come up with to transform this to reality.

Develop an Action Plan

So, if your dream is about winning a gold medal what are you going to do about it?

Now we can begin to formulate specific action plans. Who will do what and when?

Without an action plan, there is a real risk that the possibilities will remain just that – possibilities!

We will move to discuss Conversations for Action in Chapter 12.

In conclusion:

- Conversations for possibilities are great for shifting moods.

- The focus is on what can be done in a situation, or on moving towards a goal.

- Physical setting, timing and body postures impact on the effectiveness of our conversations.

CHAPTER 12: CONVERSATIONS FOR CO-ORDINATING ACTION

A conversation for co-ordinating action is almost a science in itself. I am surprised that we ever get it right and effectively co-ordinate action. You might already be listening to us making the simple complex, or as you continue to read you might be listening to your self-talk saying this is obvious or too complicated. Once again we ask that you suspend your assessments and let it unfold in order to reflect at the end of the chapter on what you can take from it.

What we will develop for you is a conversational map of how to chart your way through what is an everyday conversation. We claim that a key role in living is being able to make effective requests.

In learning the Ontological approach, Julio Olalla quoted Werner Erhardt as saying, "You show me someone who is suffering and I will show you someone who is not making enough requests." Since listening to this I have found extensive evidence to ground this assessment.

Many people feel they cannot make requests, while others feel they should not have to – it should be obvious! So as unhappy parents, maybe you are not making enough requests. The whole world is a network of help just waiting to be tapped into.

Mastering conversations for co-ordinating action is critical for parents. We need to make clear requests, gain commitments, set boundaries for children, plus mentor and coach our children into doing the same. Some of the time we do not get it right when expressing our requests and we blame the other. We cannot emphasize how critical a skill this is in the role of parenting. We don't make clear requests, we don't listen for acceptance, then we blame our children and others for not doing what we asked of them!

We want to re-visit an important dichotomy that has a significant impact on moods, relationships and future action and behaviours, that being the 'moving away from' versus 'moving towards'. By moving away from we mean statements like, "Naughty boy" (a light smack?), "Don't do that", "Stop that." The focus is on stopping a certain behaviour or action but does not lead to future actions, just a void. What is more, implied and/or explicit, is a negative mood and punishment, and potential for damage to relationships and possible problems for children such as low self confidence, low self esteem, aggression, anxiety and stress, just to mention a few. By moving towards, we mean making requests about future actions – moving ahead. This might mean reframing some of your 'moving away from'.

Conversations for Co-ordinating Action

The Elements of an Effective Request

Before we outline all the current elements we have identified, we hasten to add that we are not suggesting you must always think carefully about all of them before making any request. However, with very important requests, where careful preparation is observed to be warranted, this could be a good starting point.

If you had to always think carefully about all the elements before making any request you would probably throw this book into the corner at this point, or you would become reluctant to make any requests. What we are suggesting, however, is for you to start by going back and checking the list of thirteen elements to see what, if any, was missing in your request, when you don't get what you have requested, before you blame your partner, child or others.

Some of you might already be reluctant to make requests of others, at least in certain contexts. Some of you might also say to yourself, or to others, that, "I shouldn't have to ask!" Well, given that we are all different observers of the world, what may be obvious to you may not be obvious to others. This is particularly relevant to children.

There are thirteen elements that we have identified as worthy of consideration when making an effective request. These elements are all interlinked, some more so than others, and we are 'teasing them apart' here to make the elements more distinct and observable. The same elements apply also to making an offer.

The difference between a request and an offer is where the responsibility for the action lies. For a request, the responsibility for the action resides with the person who accepted the request. The responsibility for the action with an offer resides with the person making the offer. Most of what I discuss for the remainder of this chapter applies equally to both requests and offers.

The Thirteen Elements

1. **A listener**

> When you make a request, do you have someone listening to you? Given that we have already identified we have two conversations, a private one and a public one, is this person listening to you or to their own conversation? ("I wish he would be quiet so I can read

my book.") Some might hear the words but not be listening. We might even be guilty of accepting the request without listening and then not know what it is we have committed ourselves to! Someone who is very emotional is unlikely to be in a good space for listening to you. Children can be so caught up in what they are doing they may not be listening to you.

2. **A speaker**

How can you have a request without a speaker? Common statements that I hear frequently are, "I shouldn't have to ask!", "You should know what I want!", "It must be obvious what is needed right now!", "It is obvious to me, why not you?" But what has that got to do with 'a speaker'? What about dirty dishes being left everywhere, so you make lots of noise as you collect them? What about when you are crashing dishes in the kitchen with the dishwasher being packed or unpacked, and neither your partner nor teenage children take any notice? For a truly effective request, we must have a speaker – you must make a request! We are all different observers of the same world and what is so obvious to one is not obvious to the other.

3. **What is missing?**

When you master your awareness you become aware of what is missing and is causing you a breakdown, remembering that the distinction of a breakdown is anything that breaks the transparency of the moment for you. It may be as simple as you being thirsty so what is missing is a drink. Or it may be you are finding yourself becoming quite stressed about dirty dishes being left for you to clean up. When we become mindful and aware of what is happening to us we can simply ask, "What is missing?" We have found this very simple question so profound in times of high pressure and stress. Once we become aware of what is missing the answer is simple – make a request!

4. **Context**

My friend Julio says to me, "Mr Graeme, I have a request." *Ah, ha,* I think, *he is going to ask me to do something,* and I am then listening! My wife might say, "I have something important to ask you. Is now a good time?" Then I am listening! You might also need to set the context so that the person is on the same topic as you. Has someone ever made a request of you that is totally out of context with what you were thinking or doing? When this happens it is like they are making no sense. It is also difficult to understand the nature of the request and the concern of the person making the request. Without this knowledge or understanding, the person is unlikely to become involved in helping us to take care of our own concerns. The context helps develop a shared understanding. If we go back to 'moving towards' versus 'moving away from', instead of yelling, "Stop banging your toy on the floor", we could take a moment to explain what your needs are right now. Remember that we all have special needs.

5. **Future Action**

What action do you require when making this request? What do you want the other person to do? It is important that you are clear about the future action you require before moving into some of the next elements. Sometimes this is simple and obvious, other times not so. If what is missing is action to clear away dirty dishes, then that is quite clear, but what could the future action be regarding banging the toy on the floor? Playing quietly?

6. **Shared background**

When two people come together in a relationship they initially have very little shared background. It starts with all sorts of simple things such as how and when they like their tea or coffee. As they spend more time together they develop what we call a shared background of obviousness. Once developed, a shared background can result in saying something as simple as, "Would you like a cuppa?" Once you know, it is easy!

If children from a previous relationship are involved, then much work has to be done to develop a shared background of involvement around parenting.

New parents are constantly working towards shared backgrounds with their babies and young children. One trap here for parents of very young children is to assume too early that their child does not like a certain food. If they continue to refuse a certain food after many trials then you can accept they don't like it.

Many a request or offer has gone wrong because we have assumed there was a shared background of obviousness, when there wasn't. For example, your child may have a friend over to visit and you make a request of both children to wash their hands and get ready for lunch, but the visitor will not have the same shared background as your own child. (Where do we wash our hands? Where is the soap? Liquid soap? Block of soap? Which towel?) We now move onto conditions of satisfaction or standards, which, over time, become a shared background of obviousness.

7. **Conditions of Satisfaction**

In making requests, the conditions or standard that will satisfy you need to be clearly understood and shared. What are the boundaries? We can't emphasize too much the importance of you both agreeing to the standard and/or boundaries, both for the sake of your relationship and for clarity with your child or children. How broad or narrow are you both going to set the boundaries? How high is the bar? When you made a request and the standard was not what you expected, did you reach a clear shared understanding of the standard required or did you assume a shared understanding? With the visiting child example, did you need to be clear that washing their hands also requires the use of soap, and wiping clean hands on a towel? In many instances we are now getting into the hard stuff. How do you chart your way through what might be obvious or not, and state clearly the standard that is expected?

8. Timeframe

Some of our clients actively oppose the idea of having timeframes, except under exceptional circumstances. We challenge them on this issue as we see timeframes as critical to managing commitments. Obviously there are times when we must request a timeframe; what we need might be critical to fulfilling another commitment to someone else. You might make a request of your son or daughter to get ready to go out by a certain time so you can meet your commitment to be at your destination on time.

Less obvious is where we make a request without a timeframe. We are left wondering when our request will be fulfilled. If you request that your child puts his toys away out of the lounge room without a timeframe, you have no grounds for complaint when the response is, "I haven't got around to it yet." You might also be left feeling you are not a high priority. As you will see when we discuss responding to requests, without a timeframe you have little opportunity to negotiate priorities.

There are certain requests and offers that are made in the context where there would be a shared understanding of the timeframe. For example, if you were at the dinner table and you made a request of someone to pass you the salad, it sounds silly if you were to put a timeframe on it. "Could you please pass me the salad in the next twenty seconds?" There exists a context and a background of obviousness. Having said this though, when making requests of very young children you may have to put a timeframe because in their minds it may not occur to them you mean now!

9. Moods and Emotions

First of all let us remind you that we are always in a mood. Secondly, emotions happen as result of an event. In addition, the right conversation in the inappropriate mood is, we claim, the inappropriate conversation. In making a request, we need to be concerned for the moods and emotions of both ourselves and the person of whom we are making the request. The concept of 'moving away from' versus 'moving towards' has a significant bearing on our requests. If I demand that my son turns the music down (moving away from) versus, "Could I please have the music quieter so I can concentrate", it requires a certain mood shift from me and may elicit a different mood and response from my son.

As a child I, Graeme, quickly learnt that there were good times to ask for things and there were not so good times. My parents both contributed to this learning as they assessed each other and advised me on when it is not a good time. In a family setting, if you or your partner are in a bad mood this impacts on all within the family (including the cat!). Children learn to know when is a good time or a not so good time to make requests.

As parents we must be able to read our children's moods to determine the right time to make requests. To make an effective request, we also need to be mindful of our moods and do whatever we need to do to shift our moods if necessary. One of the many reasons we do not advocate even a light smack is that they are mostly administered in an inappropriate mood (so it might not be light!) and it will directly impact on the (potentially long term) mood of the child. It is aggression and a form of violence, and aggression and violence can become the accepted way of being. We must also remind you that a smack is 'moving away from' and as such it leaves a void. It does not give an indication of what is desired.

Contrary to popular belief, moods don't have us, we have moods. We can choose what mood we want to be in and change it if we want to. For information on changing our moods and emotions, we refer you to the chapter on Moods and Emotions (Chapter 4).

10. **Authority**

Authority can be interpreted as our assessment of our own or others' authority. We are always assessing our own and others' authority when considering co-ordinating action with them. Children are often aware of this.

Alison, when standing in for a day as a relief teacher, requested that two little Prep girls come out from under the table and they said no. They did not give her the authority, or they assumed the power to decline. When the regular teacher made the same request they accepted the request and resumed their places.

Our assessments of authority directly impact on our predisposition to make requests or offers. For example, we may be less inclined to make a request of the head of a school than of our child's teacher.

Our assessments also directly impact on the way we make requests, the way we respond to requests, the way we manage and complete our commitment and the authority we give to their assessments about our standard and commitment. This assessment of authority also impacts on our desire to complain or not.

We see there are two main sources of authority for parents. As a parent or carer you have the authority to co-ordinate action with your children and with others who provide care or services for them. You have the authority to request what you consider is in their best interests. With the authority granted to you as a parent you have the power to make requests. The other source of authority is that of you being a perfectly legitimate, valid human being who has an equal right, as anyone else, to make powerful requests. In our work we see many people, young and old, who give away this power.

Very young children do not have much authority although I do see my grandson starting to exercise some authority and challenge his parents. Obviously at twenty months he does not know about 'authority' but he does test the boundaries.

As children grow up we, as parents, must assign more authority to them and assume less ourselves. We have seen numerous examples of people in their late teens whose parents have not let them grow up. They have been denied much of the authority that could have been granted them and their parents still treat them like young children. A key aspect of parenting is to coach your children into being comfortable and skilled at developing their authority and being able to make powerful and effective requests.

11. Mode

When we make requests, they can be soft and informal at one end of the continuum and very hard and formal at the other. For example, "Could you possibly pick up some chocolate on your way home from work", versus, "I insist that you be home by nine p.m. tonight." At one end of the continuum we assess the consequences for declining the request to be significantly less than at the other. When the policeman demands that you get out of the car it is still a request in our interpretation, but the consequences if you decline are assessed to be significantly greater than if a friend asks us.

Mode becomes more important as you will see later, when we have a need to complain. As well as being about the verb being used in the request, mode also includes non-verbal or pre-verbal aspects of language such as voice tonality, pitch, loudness, etc., and body and facial gestures including eye contact.

12. Body

I have spoken previously about how we hold our moods in our body and how, by being centred, we move to a positive mood. I invite you to reflect on what might the body of someone who is making a powerful request looks like? Maybe you could stand in front of a full length mirror and experiment with what you think would be the body of someone making a powerful request. Perhaps you could work with a friend or partner and practise shaping each other's posture into bodies of people making powerful requests. Being centred would be a good start, with feet firmly planted on the ground, your vertebrae and neck stretched and your head erect. You might also look at the body of someone making a powerful decline. Start with being centred again and if you have a right hand preference, put your weight forward onto your right foot and put your hand out like a policeman directing traffic to stop. Then look the person directly in the eyes. This is very useful to teach our children in case they are confronted by someone wanting to engage in unwanted advances or behaviour. We can stop people in their tracks with a centred and powerful decline.

13. **Trust**

Whenever we consider making a request of someone we begin by assessing if we can trust them to fulfil the commitment we are requesting of them. Equally when we have received a request or an offer, we assess if we trust them or not when deciding what our response could be. In our interpretation trust involves four assessments. These are:

- **Sincerity.** This is often the hardest one to assess and, over time, it relates to the identity that this person has created for themselves. Often in assessing this element we may rely on our intuitive or gut feeling. It relates to the question of: Does what they say match their intentions? If someone was to say they will do something for you but you observe them shaking their head, you would question their sincerity, and probably feel that it won't happen. Children are quite transparent when being insincere. We often know when they are fibbing.

- **Reliability.** Has this person been reliable in managing their commitments in the past, or have they been reliably unreliable in the past?
- **Competence.** Is this person competent to fulfil my request? You would be foolish to ask us to fix your car, but as your friends have found us to be competent parent coaches, you may be more inclined to request coaching.
- **Care.** This element revolves around the assessment that this person will take care of my concerns. For example, if I request a glass of water will they ensure that the glass is clean.

To explain how this works we will share with you a true story:

> Graeme recalls Julio Olalla using an example where he was asked by his fifteen year old daughter if she could go out in the evening to a party with her new found eighteen year old boy friend. Her father declined, to which the daughter responded, "Don't you trust me?" Julio said he thought about this carefully and replied, "I know you are sincere, you say what you mean and you are very reliable, plus you always consider our concerns. However, I assess you don't yet have the competence to take care of yourself at a party with an eighteen year old boy." His daughter accepted this.

Parents must ensure, when assessing trust in the context of making requests, that their assessments are grounded. Why? Often we make assumptions about people and these go untested. Furthermore, our actions that result from these assumptions are reinforced. To explain what we mean we will tell you another short story.

> A dad was asked by his son's local football club if someone could help out as an umpire. Well, in his mind that meant him! He knew his wife didn't know how and he assumed that his daughter would not be interested. So off he went with his son and did a stint as a goal umpire. The local club was delighted and everyone was happy, problem solved – almost! Dad had made an assumption that his daughter would not be interested. What he didn't do was check with his wife or daughter. His daughter had been umpiring football at school and loving it. Mum knew this! The daughter was really disappointed that she was not asked and, much to her father's surprise was very critical of some of his decisions, but she is now an umpire for the local football club.

Often children are very good at making declarations, to which we often respond with an offer. For example, "I'm hungry", to which we reply, "Would you like a ..." We encourage you to teach your children about making requests, so as to equip them for life in the wide, wide world.

Responding to a Request

We claim that to be effective parents and carers it is an imperative that you master the art of conversations for co-ordinating action. After making a request your role is to listen, and to listen carefully to the response. If you made a request and it was not fulfilled, and you have checked that you had all thirteen elements in place when you made the request, then the miscommunication may have occurred in the response stage. There are basically five responses to a request. The first one is the most common one and is the one we do not advocate as a legitimate response. We call it a slippery response.

A *slippery response* is where we did not get a commitment or promise. Some examples of slippery responses are, "Huh, see what I can do.", "I'll give it a go.", "S'pose.", "I'll see if I can fit it in." You have all heard them before! The only option here, in order to gain clarity about how they are responding, is to plead dumb. "I am sorry, I am not clear. Do I have a commitment or not? Do we have a deal?" In our interpretation there are four responses that lead us to being clear about the possibility of co-ordinating action and these are outlined below.

Tacit agreement is another trap we might fall into when we make a request of multiple people. We make a request of all children present in the room and assume we have tacit agreement. This can lead to breakdowns in a number of areas, none the least being: Did we have all members listening to the request? Secondly, have they all agreed? If they were not listening how could we have tacit agreement? Requests to an individual, or a group of people, must involve each member responding in some way with one of the following four responses:

1. **Accept**

    When a person accepts a request, ensure there is no doubt that the person is committing to the request. What do we mean by this? As parents we have certain authority or power over our children and they may feel that they do not have the power to respond in any way other than "yes". This does not necessarily mean that it will be done. If you begin practising this conversation, you will need to be mindful that others do not necessarily know the linguistic moves that you now have. We hope that you might teach others, but when you make requests of others who do not know, you might have to offer the next three responses.

2. **Decline**

When declining a request and when we assess the relationship is important, then we would normally give our reasons. In giving reasons we can then have conversations that may lead us into the third or fourth possible response. However, if we are confronted by a total stranger, either by telephone or in person, who may be requesting that we buy something or do something, the relationship is of no consequence and we can simply decline without offering any reasons or explanations. Most sales people are trained to get three declines. So simply reiterate, "No". After three no's they will leave you alone! We do not give them the authority or the power to have us do something we do not want to do. As mentioned previously, also consider your body in making a powerful decline. We must teach our children this for their own safety. Do not give strangers the authority to have you do something you do not want to do!

3. **Negotiate or make a counter-offer**

We see this conversational move sadly lacking in most situations, none the least being between parents and children. We see this as, in part, not understanding or having the competence to engage in this type of conversation, and, in part, it is an issue of assessments of authority and power.

I, Graeme, have said previously that if I had my time over again with my three sons I would not say, "No, I don't have time". What I did not realize then is that the message they received was that whatever I was doing was more important than them! What I now do, at the very least, is to say, "No, I am working on this at the moment, but I will help you as soon as I have finished". One of my grandsons likes trains and we took our grandchildren on a steam train ride. When we got home he immediately wanted to re-enact some features of the day with his train. It was late and he was tired, so he was asked to get in the bath. When he showed his displeasure, we negotiated a ten-minute play time before his bath, which he readily accepted. I am sure his mood, and the mood of others, would have been different during bath, dinner and bedtime without this negoitiation!

4. **Commit to commit later**

Your son or daughter makes a request of you to do something in the future, say next weekend, and you are in the middle of doing something that requires your immediate attention. If you can't check the family diary or check with your partner, what do you do? It is not taking care of their concern if you make the typical response of, "Don't bother me now!" What would be more effective is to say, "I am in the middle of doing something right now, but I will come back to you in about twenty minutes and let you know." Notice that an effective commit to commit later has a timeframe. Of course, when you get back to them you can use any of the above four options. You can accept,

Conversations for Co-ordinating Action

you can decline (and give reasons as your relationships are important), you can negotiate or make a counter-offer, or you may have to again commit to commit later. E.g. "I will have to get back to you again after four p.m. when I can check with your mum/dad."

When responding to a request – remember that we see demands as requests – we believe it is useful to acknowledge you have special needs and so do your children. We find it helpful for children to understand that we all have special needs at some times, so at times we might need to negotiate around these needs. If you are resting you could explain to your child that your need right now is to rest, while also acknowledging that they have a need which you will attend to by a certain time. If they are being noisy you could set the context of your special need right now and request some quiet time. You could also indicate that they can go back to being noisy at a certain time. Obviously you can make only simple requests of young children, but by generating an understanding of everyone having special needs, you are investing in the future for both you and your children. Once your children become teenagers this can potentially minimize some of the tension that occurs. For example, your special need might be that you want to know when you can expect them home and for them to advise you if they are going to be late. This is because you are concerned, and worry about them. At the same time, parents can acknowledge that their teenagers' special needs are to develop more independence and to have a good time.

Now a brief word on children and strangers. We have found that it is not helpful to teach children to not talk to strangers. Why? Well there are predators out there for sure, but there is also a much larger network of help available for children to tap into. If we teach our children how to powerfully say "NO" to anything they do not want to do, plus how to make effective requests of people they assess they can trust, then we consider they will be much safer.

Consider the situation where a person is trying to abduct a child in a busy shopping centre. The child is terrified but does not know how to conjure up sufficient power over the situation, and has been thoroughly trained to not speak to strangers (not the abductor nor anyone else!) The security guards, shopkeepers, and other mums and dads, are all part of a network of help that a child could assess as trustworthy and ask for help. Even if alone in the street they could still exercise a powerful NO and go to the nearest house to request help.

A common response to the course we advocate is that it is all obvious. Why then is the espoused theory not generally observed in practice, either by ourselves or others? As we have stated previously, we are making you aware of the obvious in the hope that you will practise these conversations until they become habits, become transparent. Making and managing commitments is the key to effective parenting and family communication. Now that we have made effective requests and gained commitments, the next step is managing commitments.

Managing Commitments

When we make a commitment we put our trustworthiness on the line. When we don't keep our commitments, our identity and other people's assessments of our trustworthiness, is impacted upon. From early childhood we have probably suffered the wrath of our parents when we didn't keep our promises.

Conversations for Co-ordinating Action

What we mean by managing commitments is conscientiously working towards keeping our commitment. However, in all domains of life, things happen that make it difficult, if not impossible, to keep all our commitments.

People are reluctant to have conversations with people to whom they have made a commitment, when they realize it is unlikely they will be able to meet the commitment. Why is this so? Is it because of the memories of reactions by our parents when we were young or maybe the reactions of others in the past, such as school teachers, or maybe because we hate to admit defeat or failure?

Conversations about managing commitments have to occur as soon as there is an awareness that a commitment will not be kept. How much less worry would there be if your teenagers were to ring and say that they had missed a train and would now be on the next? Have you created a family environment that bad news is not welcome? Do you foster this with others at home and at work?

A simple example is when I am driving to a meeting in a cafe to meet a couple of parents, and there is an accident on the freeway that has caused traffic to come to a standstill. Do I telephone straight away to advise that I might be late or do I wait until I know I am going to be late, or do I wait until I am already late? As soon as I become aware that I might be late I make the call. Not only do I take care of the couple, but I also lower my stress levels and drive in a more relaxed manner.

As an example, your children wanted to go to the zoo and you made a commitment to take them the following weekend. Now something else has come up, which means the zoo visit cannot happen that weekend. Your children will accept the news more readily if you tell them straight away, rather than the night before, and make a counter-offer of a trip to the zoo the weekend after. It will mean just a little longer to wait.

We cannot emphasize too strongly that, as a parent, it is important for you to establish the climate (mood) where people feel comfortable having conversations with you about managing commitments, and ideally this would start at a very early age.

The responsibility for managing commitments sits with everybody. We have seen some truly remarkable outcomes where families have felt comfortable to have these conversations as soon as they are aware of the possibility that a commitment might not be kept. If our children tell us as soon as a school project or assignment 'goes off the rails' it is more readily 'put back on the rails' than if we find out weeks later and we have to go back to retrace our steps. In addition, there is far less stress if dealt with straight away. If I go back to my simple example of a traffic jam, once I have made the call I can relax rather than constantly worry whether I will make it, and possibly not drive as carefully as I might normally.

A further key part of managing commitments is to request reports on progress. If, as a parent, you find yourself being a 'snoopervisor', interrogating your children to find out about progress and commitments, you are locked into a dance that has with it a negative mood. "How are you going with your school science project?" "Is this going to be on time?" "Have you done your homework?" This is most often followed by directing. "OK, now do this." "Get this done first." "Fix this." If your children understand the importance of taking care of your concerns and keeping you informed it creates a different mood. The important thing to focus on is the outcome with the homework. As we have stated previously, different children will work in different ways. It is not when they do homework, but that it is completed within the timeframe (or that they manage their commitments).

As a parent who is also responsible for managing moods, rather than 'snoopervising', you can make a request of how and when you want to be kept informed. The natural response when you are kept informed is to thank them or acknowledge their progress etc. This acknowledgement and thanking is also an important, and yet often forgotten, part of conversations for action. When someone has completed a task asked of them, they are looking for acknowledgement and appreciation of a job well done. When it happens, it creates a positive mood. When the acknowledgement is not there, the mood can sour, and resignation can also occur. "Why bother doing things when my efforts are not appreciated anyway?"

A Graeme example:

> I was working with one single mum who had a son in his late teens, and they were both locked into battle over how he spent his time studying for his degree. She thought he was wasting time and not getting his assignments done and wasting her money. When I got her to 'get off his case' and have him tell her how he was going with assignments, his mood changed. He happily

reported that instead of his usual being late with assignments he had actually finished two weeks ahead of time.

When a commitment is completed this needs to be conveyed as well. If I made a request of Alison to have a conversation with a potential client by Friday and she accepted my request, come next week I am left wondering if the conversation happened and what was the outcome. I would most likely call Alison and interrogate her. "Did you talk with the potential client? What happened? What did she say?" Conversely, if Alison was to call me to say they had the conversation, my first response would be to say "Thank you". The conversation has started in a far different mood.

If your partner acts like a 'snoopervisor' maybe you are not taking care of their concerns and keeping them informed. Break the cycle and inform them before they inquire. When you make requests of your children, also add a request for them to keep you informed. When making requests of anyone, you can also request that they report back to you once the request is completed.

Once completed we make an assessment as to whether this is what we requested. If it is, then an appropriate acknowledgement is warranted. If it is not, then I would start by reviewing how effective was my request. Was I clear with the standard? Did I assume a certain background of obviousness? Did I have a listener? Was their commitment a 'slippery' one? If the finger is pointing at you then a further request may be necessary. As an effective parent, we must manage our emotional reaction until we have at least looked at our own contribution to the breakdown.

Complaining Effectively

If we believe we made an effective request, there was an acceptance to our request, but the commitment was not kept or at least not to the standard requested, then we have grounds to complain.

There are four steps to effectively complaining. These are:

1. **Establish that all parties agree there was a commitment**

    When we make a request and allow a slippery response to get by us then we get blown out of the water at this step. "Oh, I didn't agree to that." If I let someone respond with a "huh" to my request, they can rightly claim they didn't make a commitment.

2. **Agree that it has not been kept**

    This step can be the subject of a lot of conversation. Most often conversations for stories and assessments (and whingeing and whining). Often this is about blaming other people or other things that may have prevented them from fulfilling their commitment. At this stage you may have grounds for a further complaint, especially if you had a commitment that they would manage their commitments and inform you the moment they became aware of the possibility of not being able to keep the commitment. In many instances this step requires that we ground the assessment using all the five steps as outlined in Chapter 10.

3. **Have a conversation about the damage that has resulted from the commitments not being kept**

   This step is essential to ensure commitments are effectively managed in the future. This step is critical. In our observation, few people engage in discussing the damage as a result of not keeping commitments. Damage can be done in the areas of:

   - Your ability to keep your commitments
   - Trust (reliability, competence, sincerity, taking care of your concerns)
   - Identity – theirs, yours
   - Relationships

4. **Make another request**

   This is where we need to consider the mode. We must consciously consider how we make the request. We imply that the consequences of not accepting the request and/or not fulfilling this request will have more severe consequences. In making another request you are moving away from the descriptive conversations of the first three steps into taking some action to address the breakdown.

Making a complaint in a family environment

Let's go back to our request that our teenage son lets us know if he is not going to be home by the agreed time. When he does finally arrive late, you are out of your mind with worry and want to lash out at him. You also realize he has been drinking and it is not going to be an appropriate time to have a conversation. You make a request that you want to talk about the situation at lunch time tomorrow. By then you may be in a more appropriate mood! During this conversation you both agree that you had an agreement that he call you if he was held up. He has lots of excuses – he just lost track of the time, he accuses you of being overprotective and interfering and so it goes on. You describe the impact of his behaviour on you – you were worried sick, you feel you cannot trust him when he is out with his friends. You acknowledge his special needs and remind him of your special needs. You make another request that he texts or calls you if he is going to be home later than the agreed time the next time he goes out, and add a consequence for breaking that commitment.

Making Offers

A key part of our role as parent coaches is to maintain relationships with our clients, customers and contacts. We do this for many reasons. However in the context of making and managing commitments, we listen to how things are, what are the breakdowns for people, and if we think we can be of assistance we will make them an offer. We find it most effective and conducive to our style to listen for the breakdowns and make offers rather than try to sell our services when we don't know if people have a need to buy them.

The Five Linguistic Acts

Over the preceding chapters we have outlined what we call the five linguistic acts. These are:

1. Assertions
2. Declarations (including assessments)
3. Requests
4. Offers
5. Promises (commitments)

The above distinctions are critical if you wish to be precise with your conversations, model conversations that will serve you and your children well and be more effective as parents, grandparents and carers.

In conclusion:

- Conversations for co-ordinating action or making and managing commitments is the third of the three key types of conversations that are required in all areas of life.

- As stated previously, the key to successful relationships is to ensure a good balance of all three.

- We see families as networks of commitments and the success depends on the rigor of the conversations, and the moods and emotional contexts in which they occur.

CHAPTER 13: IDENTITY

Identity has to do with the way we show up in the world. Everything that you say and do, your moods and emotions, the clothes you wear, your appearance, your grooming and your body shape, all impact on your identity.

The moment you come in contact with someone, your identity is on show. When it comes to parenting, creating a positive identity for both yourselves as parents and for your children is critical for success in the world. You might consider how you show up when you go down to the corner store in your old sloppy stained track suit. I am concerned for the identity I am creating by showing up in this way. My identity relates to the various roles I play in life; as a son or daughter, father or mother, brother or sister, or as someone who might be an offer to others to assist them with their breakdowns.

What do we mean by all this? How does your identity affect how your family members feel about you? If you saw one of us dressed very sloppily would you consider us as potential parent coaches? This also applies to your children. Your young adult children may well go down the track of adopting certain styles which challenge you, but we would say that if you have brought them up to consider their identity then they have made an informed choice. In our work, we find that many people do not consider this distinction of identity and its impact on others.

There is no damage to your identity if you appear in neat casual gear, but the potential damage to your identity is greater if you appear sloppy. You don't know what other members of the family or people you come in contact with might think when they see you in a very sloppy, untidy way. Some of you might be thinking this is not right. "I would not care if I saw him or her dressed sloppily at the weekend" – or would you? What would that chatter in your head be saying? When you are talking about others, what assessments do you have? I readily accept that appearance may not impact negatively on your impression of others, but, for some, the potential is there. If you do impact on someone negatively and they start to engage in stories and assessments with others, very quickly your identity has become tarnished.

Identity

For us this topic presents us with more questions than answers on a daily basis. We do not profess to be masters in this area, nor do we have all the distinctions that allow us to be able to effectively intervene, which is why we will call upon the services of one of our strategic alliances, Jon Michael, CEO of Image Group International Pty Ltd. If you would like to enhance your identity, we invite you to consider seeking professional assistance in this area. Before I, Graeme, referred my clients to Jon I decided I needed to experience what it would be like. I am glad that I did as the process can be very confronting, and it is useful to understand this before referring people. When I took my wardrobe along we ended up with two heaps of clothes. We had one big heap that was to be recycled and a small heap that I could keep. The pain, however, was very worthwhile for me. We all like to receive the occasional compliment. I am not sure if it was indicative of my wardrobe but I do not recall receiving compliments in the past, at least certainly not to the degree I do now. My wife also threw herself on the mercy of Jon and she frequently conveys to me the compliments she receives.

The colours of your clothes are critical for bringing out the best in your appearance and identity. There are certain colours that suit some but not others. A key starting point is to have guidance as to the colours best suit you. When Jon put a colour chart around my neck I immediately looked like a clown. Then when he put one of the other charts around my neck I was amazed at how it blended. So I now have a range of colours that I can, and cannot, wear. Out of this range of suitable colours I can choose what to wear for the day and/or events. Jon was able to show me how white shirts drain the colour from my face, but I required some white shirts for when I play in one of the bands. The white shirts I now have are subtly off white and most people would not pick it, but I look alive!

As a parent you may intuitively know what looks good on your children and what doesn't. When you know your colours and those of each of your children it makes buying clothes so much easier. Hand me downs and/or second hand clothes can be handy for kids to play in around the home, but when it's about going out we encourage you to think a little differently.

We have seen many people who have been affected by going out in 'hand me downs'. They have created many different stories about this. Many say they hate being given them. For many it has had an impact on their assessments of self worth, self confidence and self esteem.

Identity

Clothes are part of our identity and they must be a good fit. At the start or end of each day, I look towards the forthcoming day in relation to who I will be meeting and for what purpose, and this determines what I will wear for the day. I also consider how I want to feel for the day, which also impacts on what I will wear. If I assess any snippets of negative moods I choose clothes to suit the mood I want to be in as well.

We advocate that, when old enough, children should be encouraged to choose what they want to wear and for them to consider what clothes for what occasions. If they have been handed down, observe how often they get chosen.

Even when we are working from home - our business is home based – we will wear smart casual as we find if we dress too casually, our attitude and mood can be too casual. I find this also has an effect on my telephone conversations and I am sure people are able, at some level, to listen to the difference.

When going out socially, I now consider who I will be with, how I want to feel, how I want my wife to feel, etc. This all determines how I will dress. I did think I did all this in the past but with the lack of distinctions around colours and clothes, and what I experience now, I obviously was not making the best of my identity. I now dress for success!

Posture is a key part of identity and feeling good about the clothes we wear can have an impact on posture. We are also acutely aware of being centred and the impact this has on our moods and identity. Being centred can be referred to as walking tall.

Imagine a sky hook attached to the top of your head that is pulling you up and if you don't stretch your vertebrae and neck your feet won't touch the ground. Not only is it virtually impossible to be in any mood other than very positive, it also has a major impact on your identity. It can make the difference between being noticed or being almost invisible. When you walk into a room and you are centred, people will notice you and want to hear from you. If you have injuries or physical disabilities that prevent you from being fully centred, then do take stock of yourself and ensure it is only these that are preventing you from being centred.

In other words think and feel positive, walk tall in your own way and allow yourself to show up. Some of our posture reflects the mood we are in and the assessments we hold of ourselves. Being centred can override these. Notice the people that capture your attention - are they centred?

I, Graeme, don't think I will ever forget the man I observed crossing the street in Alice Springs. He was aboriginal, he walked tall and erect, he looked to be a proud and confident man. He looked good and certainly caught my attention. We have seen young people who have their head down, round shoulders and bent backs. They come to us with issues about themselves, and this also results in them having issues physiologically with pain in the neck and lower back. The head is quite heavy and when we walk with head down we are defying the laws of gravity and putting a lot of strain on our neck and spine. So there are good reasons for you to be centred and for you to assist your children.

Grooming is also very important. Wearing the right clothes in the right colours is not enough if they are showing signs of wear, or are not clean and well pressed. Shoes must be clean and if they are becoming down at heel or sole, either throw them out or get them repaired! Nothing looks worse than men or women, boys or girls, wearing shoes that are looking worn out. This also applies to accessories such as belts, handbags, compendiums etc. where the leather is cracked, scratched or simply worn out.

Be careful of the identity that you or your children might look worn out! We hasten to say here that this is not about making your children clean their shoes, rather it is about your children understanding about identity plus how they feel when dressed well.

Next we come to how you wear your clothes. Once again we say they must fit. Not too tight or too big unless it is fashionable. If you are like me, Graeme, and find it a continuous challenge to manage your weight, then seek some guidance regarding what clothes to wear and how to wear them to flatter you.

My friend, Jon, is not backward when it comes to hair either, for both men and women. I never cease to be in awe when I see the positive transformation in people after changing the way they have their hair. To the men who have beards, beware! Are you mindful of what this may convey? I, Graeme, had a beard for over 30 years, and despite advice from Jon, I kept it. I only shaved it off because I had to be able to wear a dust mask and gas mask with a particular consulting job I was doing. Only after it came off did I find out how people viewed me.

Social Etiquette has always been crucial for establishing new relationships, both socially and in business. We are not about to embark on all the ins and outs of etiquette as there are many good books on the subject, but I will take the opportunity to point out some of the big detractors for you and your children. When you meet someone, look them in the eye and smile and encourage your children to do the same. This will be particularly helpful if you have children who have an introvert temperament. When shaking hands, use a firm hand, not a limp hand or a bone crusher, and once again encourage your children to do the same.

If you eat fast then pace yourself to others and don't put your knife and fork together until others are finished. If you do, this is the sign to the waiting staff to take your plate away even if others have not finished. So what is wrong with this? It is considered bad grace as others feel under pressure to finish. Obviously don't talk with your mouth full. Know when to use what cutlery and how. We observe some children and young adults who observe these simple rules and they are a delight to be with.

For parents, if drinking wine, once again pace yourself with others and don't drink it as though you are dying of thirst. Be mindful of the identity you are creating with others at the table including your children. When you are filling a glass you fill it to the waist of the glass which is where the glass begins to curve to the top. You do not fill it to the top and you must ensure others have been topped up before serving yourself. As your children become older they may want to pour the wine and if this happens then spell this out to them as well.

Speech is something we engage in all the time, mostly transparently, and it has a major impact on our identity and that of our children, both positively and negatively.

Identity

Record yourself speaking and then play it back and notice things like dropping your endings. Notice if you are sloppy with the pronunciation of some words. The um's and ah's. Notice the habitual words or phrases that creep into your speech or that of your spouse and children.

One of my colleagues pointed out to me that I repeatedly prefaced my assessments with "I guess". I knew that it was going to be difficult for me to break this habit as the first thing I said to him was: "I guess you are right!" Other examples I hear that come to mind include: "trust me", "in fact", "n that" and "actually".

There are many more examples but I think you know what I mean. Who cares, you ask? If I go back to my example with "I guess", I was creating an identity of being wishy washy, coming across as not being sure of my knowledge and skills.

We all want the very best for our children and the way they speak has a dramatic impact on the possibilities for them. A person who repeatedly says "trust me" or "in fact" could be conveying to people that maybe you should not trust them.

One big no-no for me in use of speech is assuming familiarity, especially in public, without permission. For example, do not use nicknames or surnames with 'y' on the end without the individual's permission. I, Graeme, repeatedly get a 'y' on my surname which is generally okay for two reasons. One is that the original pronunciation was more like that and secondly, most people know that I am okay with it. It does grate on me when someone I have just met or am not particularly close to assumes they can call me that. It is as though I have that name reserved for close friends. If you have a friend who you call by their surname with a 'y' on the end, that is generally a sign of a certain level of friendship. Sometimes at least, it may not be acceptable for your children to call your friend that.

Finally we think we should rise above the need to swear, at least not endlessly, and is swearing what you want to model for your children? You could unintentionally be limiting your children's opportunities in the world by having them get into this habit.

Humour needs to be used with caution. Very little humour is innocent of the expense of others. If we think about the claim that whenever we speak we speak from some concern, ask yourself before you engage in humour, "What is my concern in saying this?" In Australia, we have a culture of 'down under, tall poppy, don't get too big for your boots', and much of our humour reflects this. What is the concern? The 'tall poppy syndrome' is a fear that you will get more than me. Humour and jokes often offend or hurt at some level. They do nothing to enhance your identity, and jokes directed at your children can be particularly harmful.

Moods I have discussed previously. However our basic moods in life have a major impact on our identity. If you are predisposed to negative moods and emotions, people will be less inclined to listen to you and even less inclined to engage with you. No one willingly wants to engage with someone who is constantly in a negative mood as we are more concerned for our own safety at a very fundamental level.

As also stated previously, moods are contagious. Unfortunately it seems that negative moods are more

Identity

contagious so your bad mood will travel faster than the speed of light through all who know you. Do you want your children to become this way?

If, as good parents, we focus on what could be and move towards things being different, then how could we not be in a more positive mood? For example, if someone is deliberately sulking, they likely want to punish, rather than solve a problem. What is wrong with punishment you ask? Punishment is a good way of making sure that certain simple, or straight forward, behaviours are not repeated by offenders or others.

Nature has its way of teaching some of these. If we touch a hot plate we learn quickly not to touch it again.

One of the unexpected down sides of punishment is that the punishment will most likely have people avoid the task as well, especially in any behaviour that is more complex. For example, if a child is punished for going to run across the busy street, what have they learnt? Don't cross the street! When it comes time to teach children how to cross a busy street you will have a tougher job as they have to start by unlearning! Anxiety may get in the way of them confidently crossing the busy street. When we are with our 20 month old grandson in the car and we stop at the red light, we say to him, "Red light means we have to stop", and then when it goes to green we say, "Green light, now we can go". He knows the distinction between red and green so we are slowly shaping him for the future.

In our opinion, a good parent is also a good role model and a good coach. Children model much of their behaviour on us. I was looking at the growth of some new plants in the garden and my wife was having difficulty constraining her laughter. When I looked at my young son, who was just a toddler, he was modelling me with his hands behind his back and studying the garden intently!

A good coach brings out the best in people. A good parent brings out the best in their children. With a focus on moving towards, acknowledge any effort that was in the right direction and request different future standards, plus provide any assistance that might be required to assist the person to achieve this.

In conclusion:

- Our identity, the way we present ourselves, has a huge impact on how others see us.

- The way we dress, speak and behave has a positive or negative impact on others.

- Children model much of their behaviour on their parents.

- An important role for parents, grandparents and any adult who has a close relationship with children, is to be a positive role model.

CHAPTER 14: REFLECTIONS

In this final chapter, we each reflect on the journey we have taken to reach this point. We hope that you take the time to reflect on what has been important to you, and make some small (or big!) changes to your parenting style to better suit the needs of your unique family. Enjoy the journey, and remember there will be bumps and detours along the way!

Alison's Reflections

What would I like you to take away from this book? I can only speak for myself but in doing so I hope these ideas help in your journey as a parent.

> I would like you to take better care of yourself.
>
> I would like you to accept the gift of self-acceptance and pass this on to your children.
>
> I would like you to understand that we can only see the world through our eyes.

Reflections

Parenting is a tough job, but also the most important one you will ever have. It doesn't mean you have to be perfect, or get it right all the time. For me, a critical factor is to take care of yourself.

The parenting memories that make me cringe come from stress responses. When we are stressed we tend to lash out, to speak or act before we think and to revert to inbuilt responses that may come from how we were parented. Taking care of yourself first means you will be able to take better care of your children. In my experience, mothers with young children need regular time out to relax, rejuvenate and be themselves – without feeling guilty.

In Australia, particularly in big cities, we can be very isolated; I find this quite ironic. There is no shame in asking for help. If that help is time away from your children, or whatever it is you need to make you happier and less stressed, then it can only be a good thing. It is possible that the neighbour you ask for help will feel better about themselves too, for being seen as approachable and trustworthy.

Deep down all of us just want to be accepted and understood for whom we are, and this is the greatest gift we can give our children. It is the gift of self-acceptance. We are all legitimate, valid human beings. When we embrace the differences in each other, our relationships with our family members will go to a much deeper and more intimate level.

I met Graeme when I was very work stressed – not that I knew it at the time – and he has changed my life forever – in a good way! At our very first meeting Graeme talked about the fact that we are all legitimate, valid human beings. When I understood that there wasn't anything wrong with me, and began to learn more about myself, I was able to take better care of myself. This deeper understanding of how people 'operate' also improved my relationships with others. Instead of reacting, I am more often able to use the mood of curiosity and wonder to try to understand what is happening for that person. I can only describe it as stepping back from the situation and asking myself, "What's happening for that person?" In potential conflict situations, this is very useful!

The notion of us all being 'different observers' is also at the core of ontology. How often do we make a casual comment to acquaintances and strangers about the weather? "It's so cold today!" Yes, you may think it's cold but for someone else, it may be quite a mild day. We can only see the world as we are.

As close as we are to family members, we don't ever really know them completely. When we say let our children be who they are, we are not advocating that they are allowed to do as they please when they please. What we are saying is that we need to adapt our expectations and actions. We act and speak differently in different social situations; we need to do the same with different family members.

We claim that the better you understand and accept yourself, and your child or children, the more you will be able to trust yourself and your own intuition about parenting decisions. You will have the confidence to develop your own unique parenting style, and way of being.

With the wisdom of hindsight, I wish I had done some things differently as a parent. I wish I had known then what I know now, but life is always a journey of learning and discovery so I will no doubt be saying the same things in another ten years time.

I have been very good at self criticism; I think I am getting better at acceptance and forgiveness. I'm sure I could list all the things I did as a parent that I wish I hadn't done, and some things that I thought I did well. Having said that, I am proud of the adults who are my children – they turned out better than okay!

Graeme's Reflections

Why did I write this book? My ambition and motivation for writing this book is twofold:

One is to offer to the many parents in the world some additional thoughts, ideas and knowledge that may be helpful. I would like parents to be happier in the very important role of raising their children to realize their full potential, and as a consequence to also be happier. I think we have more than adequately covered this in all the previous chapters and in Alison's reflections.

The second and even more ambitious motivation for me is to have an impact on the world being a happier place. As I sit here today writing, there are people in the world killing each other. In my interpretation, this is primarily because two people or two groups believe they have the truth about something – be it religion, race, politics or whatever, and each is demanding the other obey or be punished and/or obliterated.

We are all human beings and we are all more similar than we are different. We must learn to embrace the diversity and to extend love and care to each other. We must also stop to reflect on how any of us can be sure that what we are fighting over is the truth. Surely if the situation has it that there are two people or groups holding a different truth, one or both cannot be privy to the truth! Part of the problem, as I see it, is that our thinking has been influenced by our significant others, people who have had a major input into our thinking, such as parents, teachers and others. We have been brain washed into believing some things to be true.

As adults we must question our thinking and be able to have conversations with others to get closer to what may be true. Consider these questions:

1. Is this the truth?
2. Is our thinking and speaking of our version of the truth blinding us to what else might be so?
3. Do you really think the creator of the universe wants us to kill each other over different versions of the truth?
4. Are you influencing your children (brain washing?) to be at war with other children in the playground, or in the street, because of their skin color, religious beliefs etc.?

Our brains are wired for survival in the wild. So we think in packs to survive and/or get food and to fend off others for scarce resources. If we look at the world today we can see evidence of this still and predict future conflicts over scarce resources.

In recent years much has been written about the plasticity of the human brain and that if we change our thinking we might also be able to change our brain structure (our hard wiring so to speak) and even our DNA! We have witnessed some evidence of intelligent conversations in positive moods, resolving some global issues peacefully.

So are we equipping our children to be happier and able to have constructive conversations in a world which is moving towards a global economy and multiculturalism?

Maybe, just maybe, through conversations we can identify the best parts of each version of the truth and design an even better version of what might be true.

Designing a better future for our planet is in all of our hands.

REFERENCES & RECOMMENDED READING

Ancowitz, N., *Self-promotion for Introverts*, McGraw-Hill, 2010

Anderson, M. & Wubbels, L., *To a Child Love is Spelled T-i-m-e*, Inspired Faith, 2004

Argyris. C., *Increasing Leadership Effectiveness*, John Wiley & Sons, 1976

Australian Parenting Conference, sponsored by ACER, February 2011

Ball, S., *A Season of Achievement: A Journal and Guide for the Effective Coaching of Junior Footballers*

Brizendine, L., *The Female Brain*, Transworld Publishers, 2007

Brizendine, L., *The Male Brain*, Transworld Publishers, 2010

Cain, S., Quiet. *The Power of Introverts in a World That Can't Stop Talking*, Penguin Books, 2012

References & Recommended Reading

Chambers 20th Century Dictionary

Covey, S., *The Seven Habits of Highly Effective People*, Simon and Schuster, 2004

Doherty, K. & Coleridge, G., *Seven Secrets of Successful Parenting*, Bantam Press, 2008

Doidge, N., *The Brain That Changes Itself*, Scribe Publications, 2008

Echeverria, R., *Learning to Learn*, 1991

Farris, D., *Type Tales, Center for Applications of Psychological Type (CAPT)*, 2000

Fishel, E., *I Swore I'd Never Do That!* Conari Press, 1994

Geyer, P., *Majors PTI™ Accreditation Course Manual*, 2009

Goleman, D., (narrated by) *A dialogue with The Dalai Lama. Destructive Emotions and How We Can Overcome Them*, Bantam Books, 2003.

Grille, R., *Parenting for a Peaceful World*, Longueville Media, 2005

Grille, R., *Heart to Heart Parenting*, ABC Books, 2008

Human Synergistics LSI and Circumplex.

Irwin., J. & de Vries, S., *Parenting Girls in the 21st Century*, Pirgos Press, 2009

Kelly, G. & Murrell, A., *Values Work in Acceptance and Commitment Therapy*.

In *Mindfulness and Acceptance*, The Guilford Press, 2004

Laney, M. O., *The Hidden Gifts of the Introverted Child*, Workman Publishing Co Inc, 2005

Lawrence, G. D., *Finding the Zone: A Whole New Way to Maximise Mental Potential*, Prometheus Books, 2010

Lawrence, G. & Martin, C., *Building People, Building Programs*, Center for Applications of Psychological Type (CAPT), 2001

Lipton, B H., *The Biology of Belief*, Hay House Inc, 2008

Martin, P., *Making Happy People*, Harper Perennial, 2006

Maturana, Humberto D., *The Tree of Knowledge*, Shambhala, 1992

McCarthy, S., *Childhood Origins: Influences on the Circumplex Styles*, Human Synergistics International, 2006

McKay, P., *Parenting by Heart*, Penguin Group (Australia), 2011

McCarthy, S., Chairman of Human Synergistics, seminar on Family Systems, Melbourne, 2011

Myss, C., *Invisible Acts of Power*, Free Press, 2004

Pease, A. & B., *Why Men Don't Listen and Women Can't Read Maps*, Pease Training International, 1998

Penley, J., *Mother Styles*, Da Capo Press, 2006

Preuschoff, G., *Raising Girls*, Finch Publishing, 2004

Rao, A. & Seaton, M., *The Way of Boys: Promoting the Social and Emotional Development of Young Boys*, Harper Collins, 2010

Sanders, A. F., *Towards a Model of Stress and Human Performance*, ActaPsychologica, Volume 53, Issue 1, April 1983, Pages 61–97

Shaw, Dr P., *Development of Cortical Surface Area and Gyrification in Attention-Deficit/Hyperactivity Disorder*, Biological Psychiatry, 2012; 72 (3):191

Tieger, P. D. & Barron-Tieger B., *Do What You Are*, Little, Brown and Company, 1992

Tieger, P. D. & Barron-Tieger B., *Nurture by Nature*, Little, Brown and Company, 1997

Tolle, E., *The Power of Now*, Hodder Australia, 2004

Zeisset, C., *The Art of Dialogue*, Center for Applications of Psychological Type (CAPT), 2006

ABOUT THE AUTHORS

Graeme Schache and co-author Alison Roberts-Wray have combined their unique knowledge and skills of parenting acquired over a combined life experience in excess of 120 years to produce this book! Through their different work experiences both have developed a passion to have the world be a happier place. Both are certified as Ontological coaches and bring much of this interpretation to you in this book.

Graeme brings his experience as a father of three boys,  grandfather, employee, manager and, since 1990, his work as a practicing psychologist and coach. Graeme is credited with bringing the ontological work to Australia; he combines this with ongoing research into childhood development to contribute to this unique work about parenting.

Graeme's previous book, *Leadership for Outstanding Results*, has been used by organisations to improve workplace relationships, productivity and business outcomes. The idea

About the Authors

that organizations are a network of conversations is a central tenet of the field of Ontology.

Alison adds to this with her wealth of knowledge and skills acquired from being a mother of a son and daughter, and from over twenty years as a primary school teacher, working predominantly with children and families in the first three years of school. Alison has worked with children and families from vast multicultural origins, which has given her insight into the rich diversity of family life that exists in Australia today.

www.ingramcontent.com/pod-product-compliance
Lightning Source LLC
Chambersburg PA
CBHW070557300426
44113CB00010B/1298